How to Remodel a Life

HOPE ANDERSEN

Copyright © 2020 by Hope Andersen

ISBN: 978-1-7347075-7-1

Andersen. Hope
How to Remodel a Life.

Edited by: Amy Ashby

PipeVine
P R E S S

Published by Warren Publishing / PipeVine Press
Charlotte, NC
www.warrenpublishing.net
Printed in the United States

*This book is dedicated to anyone who
has the courage to change their life for the Good.*

"The unexamined life is not worth living."
SOCRATES APOLOGY 38A

"*I adore Hope Andersen's life-affirming work,* How to Remodel a Life! *This beautifully written, metaphorical book is poetry in prose. Its message of redemption and continuous improvement are juxtaposed wonderfully with the physical remodeling of a house. I'm eager to give it as a gift to those who could benefit from it as much as I have.*"

-THOM HAYES, CEO, 3 LLAMA EDUCATION

"*Hope Andersen's memoir,* How to Remodel a Life, *shares with extraordinary insight the transformation possible in our lives, from confusion and obsessiveness to patience, tolerance, and love. Using the image of remodeling a home as her framework, Andersen demonstrates how she has grown to accept and love her own humanity; she suggests 'tools' in each chapter that we can use to help us discover the miracle of being wholly who we are meant to be. There is something in this book for everyone.*"

-LORNA BISHOP, CLU, CHFC, RETIRED

"*If you're going to rehab a house that's fallen into disrepair, you obviously need the proper tools. If you're going to repair a life overshadowed by addiction and mental illness, you need tools too—but you can't exactly run down to the local hardware store to find them. What you can do, however, is read this intimate, powerful, and uplifting book. Hope Andersen has transformed her own, very challenging life into what she calls 'an oasis of serenity,' and she's used the lessons she learned to create not just one, but a series of toolkits that could do the same for you. It's a remarkable achievement.*"

-MICHAEL D. LEMONICK, AUTHOR OF *THE PERPETUAL NOW*

"How to Remodel a Life *is a deeply personal account of the author's struggle with the twin challenges of a mood disorder and alcoholism. In equal parts spiritual, clinical, and practical, Ms. Andersen's narrative weaves the strands of a disjointed and deeply painful life into a coherent account of struggle and increasing mastery and joy. This book will be an invaluable resource to anyone struggling with mental illness or substance abuse, as well as to professionals treating patients with these issues.*"

-DR. DEROSSET MYERS JR., LICENSED CLINICAL PSYCHOLOGIST

Acknowledgments

I would be remiss if I did not acknowledge a number of people who have been instrumental in the writing of this book. If I have learned nothing else through my recovery in twelve-step programs, it is that *we* can do together what *I* cannot alone. Here is a big thank you to the following:

First and foremost, my immediate family—my husband Thom, son Nicholas, daughters Haldis and Kylie. Without your support and encouragement, your patience with me, and your love, this book would not be.

I am indebted to Dr. Julia Temple, who first diagnosed me as bipolar; to Mary Auhn, who set me on the right path in my recovery; and to all the doctors who have worked with me to manage my disease.

To my sisters and brothers in twelve-step recovery groups throughout the world, I am so grateful for the unity, service, and recovery that has kept me sober throughout the years. A special shout out to Dan D., who took me to my first meeting, and to Susan S., my first sponsor. To Harriet S. and Janet E., my dearest friends in the program. And to all those women who have supported and encouraged me along the way.

To Thom Hayes, of 3 Llama Press, who encouraged me to send my manuscript to Warren Publishing / PipeVine Press, and to PipeVine Press for picking it up. To Mindy Kuhn at Warren Publishing / PipeVine Press who has worked diligently with me on this and other books, and to my editor at PipeVine Press, Amy Ashby. You pushed me further than was comfortable but helped me to create something I am so proud of.

Thank you to my early reviewers and to those of you who will review the book in the future (hint hint).

Thank you, the reader, for picking up this book and making the time to read it. I hope it inspires you and leads you to joy.

Finally, but certainly not least, I thank my Higher Power for gracing my life and placing me on this journey. Thy will, not mine, be done.

Preface

Recently, I worked part-time in a bookstore. During the holidays, I couldn't help but notice how many of the bestsellers featured Joanna and Chip Gaines, stars of the popular home remodeling show *Fixer Upper*. This made me think about all the doctor's offices I have been in over the past several decades, as my husband battled—and survived—near-fatal liver cancer.

And as I have struggled with my own mental illness.

In all those doctor's offices, what always played in the waiting rooms were seasons of *Property Brothers, Flip or Flop, Fixer Upper,* or some similar home improvement show. It makes sense. America is obsessed with remodeling. We are also addicted to recovery and self-improvement. If we aren't changing our sheets, we are changing our diet and exercise, all in the hopes that we will achieve that perfect state where the world (and ourselves) looks and feels just right. This all got me thinking about remodeling not just a house but a *life,* and how there are many similarities between the two.

～

To move forward with this idea, I first had to look back. It all began back in 1981 when I stopped drinking. So much happened in the next eight years. Divorced from my first husband. Multiple job changes. Graduate school. Geographic moves. In 1989, my second husband and I were married. It was a modest wedding at my father's church in Bennington, Vermont. All we ever wanted was a simple life. Both of us were public servants—he, a wastewater treatment operator for the state of New Jersey; I, a high school English teacher. We lived in a humble apartment in Rocky Hill, New Jersey, and enjoyed competing in triathlons and being with our friends.

That simplicity lasted for about two minutes.

In 1990, our first child of three arrived; in 1991, my mother was killed in an auto accident; in 1994, my father contracted prostate cancer, and later died in 1997. That same year, my husband was diagnosed with chronic viral hepatitis C, cirrhosis, hepatic encephalopathy, and hemochromatosis. And, in 1998, I was diagnosed with bipolar disorder after having blown up our world during a manic episode, an event brought on, I believe, by my father's demise and my husband's swift decline.

The foundations of our once "simple" life were shaking; the walls were tumbling down. My husband lost his job and we relocated to Michigan, a move that would turn out to be nearly fatal for me. I had no support group in Michigan, no job, and the only two friends I'd had died by suicide—one through overdose, the other by jumping in front of a moving train. I was devastated by so many things—the deaths, my own remorse over the infidelity that accompanied my manic breakdown, 9/11 and the fear that horrific day brought with it. I spent my days sleeping when the children were at school. When they came home, I would put on a brave face and watch *The Ellen DeGeneres Show* with them, though I didn't feel like dancing.

I barely felt like living.

My husband's hepatitis C progressed, as did his liver enzymes, the result of the cirrhosis. He became increasingly listless while I struggled to find a teaching job ... that is until we were about to move again. For a time, it seemed as though our house had been built on a fault. I wondered if it would ever stop shaking.

In 2007, we moved to North Carolina. The sunnier climate and friendlier people did much to hold us together, but Thom's sickness progressed to the point that, in 2009, I was afraid we would lose him. Fear ran my life at that time—in the classroom where I now taught, in my relationships with my children, in my marriage. All I knew to do was take him to the doctors, listen to reports, and watch as he became increasingly yellow and disoriented with hepatic encephalopathy (loss of brain function due to liver disease). In 2012, I lost my job. In 2013, Thom was placed on a list for a liver transplant. By 2015, we were frustrated with waiting and sought a second opinion from the Mayo Clinic in Jacksonville, Florida. And, after two weeks of testing in the most advanced labs, they told us they could do nothing for him.

They gave my husband three months to live.

Our "house" was on fire. What could we do? The bad news came on a Monday. We left the doctor's office, threw our clothes in our bags, and drove back to Charlotte, listening to Garrison Keillor's *Pretty Good Joke Book*. We laughed and cried all the way home. On Tuesday, somber and reflective, we each reached out to our personal God. Although the prognosis was not what we had expected, and certainly not what we had hoped for, we came to accept that what must be, must be.

On Wednesday, our original hospital called and said they weren't done with Thom yet. They were keeping him on the list. Two weeks later, as a result of nothing short of a miracle, he received a new liver, "preowned" as he likes to say. It was a woman's liver, and now he cries at the drop of a hat.

I like that.

So, what does our story have to do with remodeling a life, let alone a house? Well, there comes a time in every homeowner's life when they can no longer live with black mold on the ceiling or a leaky faucet. Who knows why *that day* they take out the sledgehammer and knock down the wall to the den, or pick up the phone and dial Angie's List? Who knows why they drop to their knees and ask for help from the Universe? Whatever the reason, people make the decision to take a step toward change, the first step toward rebuilding. A house. A life.

At the onset of either "remodel," you've gotten to a point where you simply can't take it anymore. You can't keep going the way you have been going … but you can't stop either. Beautiful desperation. That's the beginning.

We reached our desperation point the morning after Thom got his sentence from Mayo. There is nothing like being told you or your loved one is going to die to make you take a serious look at your life. Even if it isn't as final as death, that sense of desperation—that you feel about your behavior, your actions, your fears—is the very thing you need to embrace in order to start remodeling your life. Once you have done this, you are ready to embark on your self-transformation project.

When you remodel a home, you must reach the point where the old structure simply does not fit your needs anymore. In rehabbing a life, the same is true. The first step to changing your life is recognizing that your old way of being is seriously flawed, non-functioning; you need help from someone, somewhere to create this new version of yourself.

ॐ

This book illustrates how I remodeled my life to get to my true self, the self that is authentically me. Chapters include topics such as allowing joy in, eradicating negative thinking, and the importance of good nutrition, self-love, and attraction not promotion. I have done my best to show you how I changed from a self-loathing, fear-driven woman who suffered from alcoholism and bipolar disorder, to a woman whose life is filled with abundance, success, love, and joy. Using my experience, strength, and hope, I will take you on a journey that has the potential to lead you to a healthier, happier version of yourself.

A word on the process: *How to Remodel a Life* is not a simple guide to be marched through from beginning to end. It is the story of my journey toward self-transformation ... with some suggestions as to what you might want to read, do, or try if you want to change your life too. There is no need to conquer one chapter and move on to the next. One thing I have learned about life is that we need to be more relaxed and fluid. So, skip around, do what pleases you.

Flow.

⌁

And by the way, my husband went on from his liver transplant to become a CPT (Certified Personal Trainer) and Wellness Coach. He is also an instructor for Livestrong, a program directed at cancer patients and survivors. For my part, in 2015, I wrote my first novel, published in 2019 as *When the Moon Winks*. A second novel, *The Book Sisters*, was previously self-published in 2017. My first book of poetry, *Taking in Air*, was released in 2018. Together, this year, Thom and I will celebrate a combined seventy-three years of sobriety. Once we made the decision to remodel our lives, life took off for both of us! It can for you too.

I wish patience and persistence for you as you embark on your remodeling. May you experience great joy!

CHAPTER 1

Clear The Dust

*A*ny contractor worth his salt will tell you that one of the most difficult things about remodeling is the dust. What's a little dust, you might ask? Dust like this is not just any dust, eradicated with a swipe of a rag and some furniture wax. This dust doesn't disappear when you blow it gently off the pages of a book. This is a pervasive dust worthy of Steinbeck. Worse than Dust Bowl dust. It is a monumental dust consisting of waste from insects and critters, gypsum from drywall, and lead particles from paint. It insinuates itself into everything from the cracks in the floorboards to your front teeth. But there is no way to prevent the dust during reconstruction. You can control it somewhat by covering floors with plastic sheets, removing furniture and other possessions from the site, and installing air scrubbers and vacuums. Still, dust will remain.

In remodeling our lives, we come into contact with *emotional* dust. When we make the decision to embark on our journeys of self-transformation, all sorts of crap escapes. At first blush, we are overjoyed! Like the cork popping from a bottle of champagne, we celebrate our change. It is not uncommon for us to feel elated, to want to shout our good news from the rooftops. "I've gone on the Keto diet!" "I've put down booze and drugs!" "I've joined a gym and hired a personal trainer!" All great things, we believe. We are doing self-help to the nth degree. Isn't everyone thrilled for us?

The fact is, some are; some aren't. Our families and friends have been through the ringer with us, our ups and downs, lies and threats. Weary of our bad behavior, they are rightfully skeptical when we come bouncing into the kitchen like sunbeams.

My own family has certainly been through it all with me. Even as a young teen, my behavior was erratic to say the least. One minute I was making cookies for the old man on the corner and writing happy notes to everyone at school, and the next I was holed up with Joni Mitchell, listening to the "Blue" album and threatening suicide. (At least those were quiet activities.) Then there were the moments when I would lose my mind altogether, screaming and throwing things until I stomped out of the house to go cool off in the woods. When I'd come back, all sunshine and happiness, I'd find that the cats had pooped on the floor and my younger sisters were crying in their rooms. It didn't occur to me that those events were a result of my actions.

Lots of debris.

In my defense, I was probably suffering from bipolar disorder, something I would only be diagnosed with in my 40s. (*Lots* of debris.) My undiagnosed manic-depressive behavior defined my relationships for many years. I was the girl who single-handedly produced a multifaceted Creative Arts Festival at my high school, never to be repeated again. I brought together artists, dancers, actors, writers, musicians, seamstresses, and chefs in an event that took over the campus on one Saturday in May. I designed and printed posters and other promotional materials, silk-screened T-shirts ... basically did it all, from soup to nuts. (To be honest, I did have some help from my amazing art teacher, Virginia Kehne) That night, after the festival was over and the rest of the school was enjoying the May Day dance, I fell asleep on my boyfriend's shoulder.

Another example of my determination (aka, mania) was one summer on Block Island, off the coast of Rhode Island. Hired as a mother's helper to take care of three little boys when I was just fifteen years old, I used one of my days off to win a bet I had made with a friend of my employer. He bet me I couldn't walk the twenty-five miles around the perimeter of the island in one day. Barefoot. I almost drowned in the channel at the very end of the trek, but I managed to survive and complete the task. I won a lobster dinner for my efforts. With me, it was always about winning.

The stories go on.

In my early twenties, I wrote a screenplay in three months and sent it to Paramount Studios. Shortly thereafter, I was summoned to California to meet with the head of the studio, Herb Jaffe. I flew to Hollywood in my new clothes, wet behind the ears and hopeful. While entering the trailer where the production offices were located, my shoe caught in a step and the heel broke. I walked down the seemingly endless corridor—a long hall with offices to the left leading to the main office at the rear—my heart beating as loud as a drum, my shoe going *ka-thwap, ka-thwap* the whole way. I was a one-woman band of nervousness as I imagined my face on fire. It certainly *felt* on fire when I saw Gene Wilder and Mel Brooks staring at me from an open door, though that might just have been the mania.

I don't remember much of the conversation with Mr. Jaffe. My mind was off somewhere else, playing out scenarios of me winning an Oscar for best screenplay and seeing my face on the cover of *People* magazine. And it was just this kind of overblown thinking that had me turn down Jaffe's offer when he asked only that I revise the last forty pages.

జ

These are all colorful stories, and there are so many more. Mania is, in its early stages, an aphrodisiac that feeds the creative spirit. But soon enough, mania deflates and depression descends, which is no fun at all.

I remember being in our family's house in Maryland. My father had been offered a job as headmaster of an Episcopal girls' school there in the mid-'60s. We lived in an old plantation home with wide porches out front for rocking chairs. The house had enough space for each of my five sisters and me to have rooms of our own, plus one for Grandma, with rooms to spare. We were brought up in that rather strange and challenging paradox; we had a Southern mansion for our home, acres to play, and horses to ride, but not enough of our parents to share with the 200 other girls who demanded their attention each day. We were not wealthy, and yet we enjoyed all the luxuries of country club living: ballet studios, soda and candy machines, film screening rooms, barns filled with horses, and limitless food. In a way, living a more fortunate lifestyle fed my diseases, because I grew up believing I was entitled to whatever I wanted. There were no boundaries, no limits. Life was one big high ... until it wasn't.

I remember one day when the rest of the family had gone to the movies or some such thing. I looked at my face in the mirror and began screaming. I could not stand the person I was looking at. I hated everything about the girl I was—the way I looked, the way I thought, the people I spent time with. The people who rejected me. All I could think to do was cover the mirrors, every mirror in the house, so I didn't have to look at myself.

My depression was an aggressive one, hell bent on annihilating me. I cut my wrists until they bled. On other occasions, I swallowed enough pills to kill an elephant. Drank myself "to Bolivia," as they say. Put myself in dangerous situations with boys and, later, men. Because I felt so empty and needy, I seemed to attract boys who wanted to hurt me, boys who cheated on me behind my back or who demanded sex.

I came very close to being raped when I was twelve years old. I was at my first "mixer," a somewhat contrived dance between one boys' school and our girls' school. There was so much anticipation in the bus driving to the dance. Big curlers, hairspray, eyelash curlers, and makeup were passed around like hookahs. We were all giddy with excitement. I had on a royal blue dress with electric green and orange piping up the side, orange tights, and blue shoes.

We filed off the bus and embarked into the dark, cold night where the boys waited for us, standing on the pavement. The other girls were chosen, one by one, and I was paired with a rather gawky young boy my own age. I dreaded the hours ahead. But then, a handsome, older, ginger-haired boy stepped up and took my arm. "You are coming with me," he said and led me off to the racquetball courts. There, he proceeded to teach me how to kiss, something I had never done before. I was grateful because I had been cast as "Emily" in our school's production of *Our Town* and I had to kiss "George." *This is good practice,* I thought, until his hands found their way under my dress and he pulled my pantyhose down. I began to panic. I was sure this was not what he was supposed to be doing. Thank God for my sister and her friend, Cynthia, who arrived just in time to stop this malicious senior boy's game.

As I cried, they told me it wasn't my fault. Still, somewhere, very deep down, I believed that it *was* my fault. That I was bad and shameful. That what that bad boy had wanted to do to me, I had somehow brought on myself. That guilt was a lie I carried with me into so many situations, not the least being the extra-marital affair I'd engage in during my manic episode in 1998.

As I have unpacked my history in these pages, shadow memories have bubbled up. I have vague recollections of being touched when I was just a very little girl by boys whom I thought I could trust. The trouble was not so much that they touched me, but that I evidently *liked* it. I was fascinated by sex from a young age. I used to stare at a photograph from the film *Tom Jones* in the school library because I was drawn to looking at the women's breasts that overflowed the tops of their dresses. I would sneak up into the boys' dormitory at school and peer around the corner to the bathroom where they showered, hoping to catch a glimpse of them buck naked. I would hide behind the sofa in our living room and watch my oldest sister kissing her boyfriend. I was intrigued by the little rubber disc I found in my mother's closet (a diaphragm), knowing it had something to do with what mysteriously went on between my parents.

When I got sober, I swore off sex all together for several years, sure that it was another addiction. I cut my hair short like a man's, restricted my diet so that I maintained 118 pounds, and took on a strong facsimile to actress Jean Seberg in the film version of Shaw's *Saint Joan*.

At least, that is what I was told.

One of my greatest joys in recovery has been letting go of the guilt I felt as a sensual being and putting sex in its proper place. Not to be over-indulged in, lied about, or used to hurt another person, but as a way to express intimacy and love. I have enjoyed many happy years of pleasure with my current husband.

As my teenage years progressed, there were darker times when I was immobilized by a doubt and fear as strong as ammonia. These emotions permeated my life. I was drawn to Scandinavian philosophers and filmmakers who seemed to understand the black mood that shrouded me. My favorite word was "*ingenting*," the Swedish word for "*nothing*." I was mesmerized by the black and white images in Ingmar Bergman's films. I felt like I could swoon into those blank, empty stares that seemed to capture so much of what was in my heart. On the lighter side, I took to wearing bright red clogs to show my kinship with Scandinavia. My mother would drive me to a special store in Pikesville just so I could purchase them. As far as I was concerned, it was wear clogs or go barefoot.

Just living with me was very hard on my family. My sisters had told me at a young age that I was adopted, that I wasn't really a member of the family at all. And I suppose their comment had some truth. I *was* different, even if related by blood. I was overly demanding and emotional. Self-centered in the extreme. A liar. A thief. A manipulator. In short, I was an alcoholic in the making. All it took was a few drinks, when I was in my teens, to get that wagon rolling down the mountain.

And then there were my friends, the few I had. How confusing for them to translate my enigmatic emotions, to decide who to love and who to hate: the star athlete, theatre queen, and super-achiever (Manic Hope) or the demanding, mercurial, and suicidal child (Depressed Hope). Although it wasn't my fault—and I am and have been so much better since getting sober, being given the proper diagnosis, and starting the right medication— the debris of that past still lingers with those who knew me then. And it lingers within me as I look back on lost opportunities, on time wasted in self-hatred, on arrogance paired with insecurity. The debris makes me so sad sometimes. But we have to look at that debris, face it, and let go of it, if we are ever going to move on into a remodeled life.

Don't make the mistake of fooling yourself into thinking that you were never the problem. Even if the debris resulted from a disease or illness, such as bipolar disorder, you still were the problem. *I* was the problem with my life. I had to cease blaming anyone or anything else. The problem wasn't my sisters shunning me or a mother who withheld love; it was *me*. I needed to accept that ... and move on.

꒰

There is a story about a man who is huddled in a root cellar with his family during a tornado, listening as the wind howls, and branches, furniture, and vehicles fly around in the storm's fury. When everything settles down and is quiet again, his family looks out on the devastation the storm has caused. His car is hanging from a tree, the roof to the house has fallen in, everything is destroyed. But the man looks at his family and remarks cheerily that the world is wonderful now that the wind has stopped.[1] That's what I was like. I was that farmer in the tornado. I was, to one degree or another, a person who had left a mess behind. I had an impact on my family and friends that was indelible, and in order to move on from the debris stage, I needed to recognize my part in the family drama.

෴

Not long ago, one of my sisters commented to me that I had ruined her life. Now while I know that is not possible, that we are each responsible for our *own* happiness, I can still see why she might feel that way. I always demanded more than the lion's share of my parents' attention and concern. My self-centeredness affected the rest of the family, whether it was my chasing after and winning the boy that same sister had wanted to date or creating a rift between my parents when I insisted on marrying impulsively, a number of years later, without their blessing. So, I may have heard a few harsh messages from people, but I must also acknowledge that I dished them out too.

The harshest message came from my boyfriend— by accident. Literally. I was in an accident just outside Providence, Rhode Island, with my friend Neria as we were returning to college from visiting friends at Yale one weekend. Most people would have been concerned by the near-fatal experience that brought them to the emergency room where they were bandaged and kept under observation. Most people would not have checked themselves out of the hospital early, against the doctor's orders. But I saw the whole incident as an opportunity to visit my boyfriend who was attending

Brown University at the time. I took a taxi to his dorm, knocked on his door, and was met by a leggy brunette wearing a white, man's dress shirt. When he saw me at the door, my boyfriend just lay on the bed, grinning. The message was all too clear.

I didn't deal with this rejection in the healthiest of ways. For many months, I harbored resentment, ate heaps of cafeteria granola and jam until I had gained fifty pounds, and slept around with anyone who showed the slightest interest in me. Those who did not, I pursued like a ravenous beast. Lest I sound like a common slut—which in fact I probably was—please understand that this promiscuity was rooted in an acute sense of aloneness and the feeling that I was unloved. While I don't now believe that nonsense, at the time, I was so wrapped up in a cocoon of self-pity, I thought I had to chase love down. (Although sex with strangers hardly qualifies as love.)

All the while, I was drinking regularly, excessively, but my excuse was that everyone around me was doing the same. Not quite. Not everyone was going into blackouts and waking up with anonymous notes on their pillow that read, "Had a great time. If you are ever at Cornell, look me up." Not everyone was crashing parties at the Black Student Union and having sex with the top dog in the crowd who called her "a tantalizing witch who had claimed his heart." Not everyone alienated old friends by insisting that they drink, smoke, and sleep with her, leaving them to later reject her friendship forever. College may have been fun for some, but to me it was a nightmare that culminated in my having to take a semester off to pull my shit together.

During that time off, I remember sitting at the kitchen table in my parents' home in Vermont. I was having a "discussion" with my mother and father about the direction my life was headed. My mother, as usual, was quiet—infuriatingly so. Because she refused to say anything, I could only imagine the disgust she must have felt for me. In reality, it was disgust I felt for *myself* ... and hopelessness.

I accused my mother of not caring. I shouted at her, "You never loved me anyway!" And like a shot, she threw her glass of whiskey across the room at me, straight at my head. It went through the window and broke the glass. I was appalled that any mother would do that to her daughter. What I could not see then was what I had done to make my mother throw that missile. Years of treating my mom like the enemy, because I felt she stood in the way of my love for my father; decades of believing she'd treated my other sisters better than she treated me; it all added up to that moment when she had simply had enough.

If only *I* had had enough. If only I had surrendered then. But it took another seven years of misery and alienation for my journey out of the depths and into sobriety to begin.

At the end of my sophomore year, I stayed at home dishing out ice cream at our local Howard Johnson's restaurant. That was a summer from hell. Of rape and running away. Rape again, which I will address at a later time. Suffice it to say, I ended up taking the first semester of my junior year off to pull myself together. I made it back to college in the second semester, in time to direct Beckett's *Waiting for Godot* with an all-female cast. I spent part of the summer of '76 in New York City at the Circle in the Square summer acting program. I believe my parents were desperately trying to channel my energies into something positive. What happened instead? I did a little acting, learned how to ballroom dance with a gay guy from class, captured cockroaches in my apartment under all the glassware, and ... had a brief affair with a married Argentinian man some years my senior. I honestly don't know what the appeal was; he had no chin and was grossly overweight, but he introduced me to a lusty red Argentinian wine called Avalar that stole my heart. To hell with the Tall Ships in the harbor. I holed up with my wine in my apartment, the alcohol's dirty, sultry thickness matching my mood of the time. That wine felt like heaven, snatching me from reality.

But it was really just rotgut. My alcoholism was what snatched me away.

My family did not approve of the Argentinian, nor did they particularly like the Irishman, twenty-five years older than I, whom I met on-stage at college the following year. It wasn't the Irishman's charisma that prompted me to marry him the spring after graduation; it was my sense of panic over how I would support myself. I am ashamed to say, I married him against my better judgement; not because I loved him, but because I felt at the time, I didn't have a choice.

Right from the start, the marriage was flawed. We both drank excessively, though he more than I. I felt unappreciated by this man who seemed so in love with himself but so removed from our relationship. I used this as an excuse to have sex with whomever I pleased. One day, while having my hair permed, I ended up in the bathroom, half a head full of curlers, having sex with my hairdresser. Another time, at a party we attended, I danced with a handsome man in a sleek suit and ended up carrying on with him at his beach house for weeks. Oftentimes, I would sneak out of the house when my husband was sleeping and go down to the Ground Round at the end of the street, where I chugged beer and picked up men. My boldness and promiscuity knew no bounds.

One day, I had made a plan to meet with a married man I was having a dalliance with. He didn't show up when he was supposed to, kept me waiting for a good half an hour. Finally, I called his wife and asked her where the hell he was. That is the kind of person I was. Self-centered in the extreme. Driven by my wants and needs.

A runaway beer truck.

Thank God that all changed when I turned twenty-five and got sober without doing any more damage, or at least not *that* kind of damage. The fact is, I had already done a great deal of damage that would take years, if ever, to repair.

Debris.

~

Now, dear reader, back to *your* family and debris. As much as our families may not like the new relationship dynamic we have created in our attempts to "self-help," they fear change even more. When the kids hear that Mom is on a diet again, they shudder, knowing this means the cupboards will be purged of any decent food, the kind they like. No more chips or macaroni and cheese. School lunches will be celery, plain yogurt, and green grapes. Why can't she just go back to being the mom who bakes Toll House cookies and invites all the other kids over to play? Not to mention what *happens* to Mom when she changes. She gets edgy and irritable. Beds must be made. TV must be turned off. Tempers flare. At least, that is the way things *have* been—in the past.

The past.

When we change, we may not actively dredge up the past, but the people around us will. How can they not? The past is all they know of us.

When I got sober in 1981, my action had a ripple effect throughout the whole family. My mother's reaction was, "Oh, now what fad are you latching on to?" And rightly so. I had tried so many things before to stop the chaos—diets, meditation groups, church, exercise. Marriage. Why should she think this would be any different? I certainly wasn't sure it would be. My decision to stop drinking was "damned inconvenient," as my father would say, because it forced him to look at his own drinking. A sober person in a room can ruin a good glass of wine ... if that drinker has an issue himself. Debris.

I have since learned that during all those years when I acted selfishly, I taught people to back away from me. When I lied or cheated, I encouraged them to view me with mistrust. My extramarital affairs hurt my ex-husband, and he, in anger, "retaliated" in kind. (A strange term to use for what we were doing to each other.) How incensed I became, and self-righteous.

When I acted the big shot, getting all puffed up inside about how important I was and how special, people shook their heads at me in dismay. I wondered why I had no real friends, even my sisters (perhaps them especially) did not consider me a friend. In reality, I only had to look at the way I had pretended I was somehow superior. Of course, the truth was I had always felt *less than* everyone else. I never had a clear and balanced image of myself.

When we start to change, we expect people to change right along with us ... but they are sometimes guarded. They are not as swift to forgive us for our mistakes as we are to ask for forgiveness. It took years, *decades* for my sisters to speak with me on the phone. Then finally, my gentle knocking, sending cards, and remembering birthdays, anniversaries (sometimes), and Christmas gifts, paid off.

One year, not too long ago, each one of my sisters visited us in our home in North Carolina. I was so happy, I wept. I no longer felt like the odd one out, but it had taken years of patient practice and trust to bring about their visits. Even now, there is still old baggage among us, but I know I have cleared up my side of the street.

If they still have issues with me, that is *their* debris, not mine.

Looking back at the past is a critical part of sorting through the debris, but wallowing in it does no one any good. We have to keep moving through the rubbish of our lives, trusting that if we just keep recycling plastic and cans, the landscape will eventually clear. Of course, litter will always reappear and require constant care, but overall the picture will be prettier, more pleasing to the eye. This cleanup is not something I suggest doing alone.

For myself, I have worked with therapists, parish priests, psychiatrists, and trusted friends on my journey. One of the truths I learned about myself from all these folks is that I take myself too seriously. In raking over the coals of my past, I was quick to brand myself with a thousand different horrible names. I knew this did nothing but keep me stuck back in the old memories, staring into the amber eyes of negativity that had long held me captive in their gaze. But I could not change, I could not even *begin* to change, if I loathed myself. It was an absolute must to learn to be kinder to *me,* the person who had done so many wrongs.

I also had to learn to sit still, instead of trying to make everything happen. One of my therapists used to say to me, "Bloom where you are planted." That makes such sense to me today. When remodeling a house, we frequently keep the old foundation. We can typically find salvageable materials that actually contribute to a stronger, newer building. In remodeling my life, I also work with what I have. And as I remodeled myself, that old me, worn and wacky as I was (and am), was the only "me" I had. So, I had to, with gentleness and kindness toward myself, sort through the debris of my life … over time. There was no race.

That cleanup took a while for me, as I had plenty of debris that needed sorting through. I had relationship debris. Financial debris. Sexual debris. It all had to be cleaned up. The most important thing about debris is to recognize that it is going to be there. The minute you start to change, people start tugging at your heels, imploring you not to. They know who you are and who you used to be. The thing is, change is inevitable. As a recovering alcoholic with a bipolar disorder, if I don't change, I might die. I have seen so many men and women perish over the years because they were unable to surrender and change. And so, change we must.

In her poem, "The Journey," Mary Oliver addresses change so beautifully. We have to persist with our change, despite objections from others, because it is the only thing we can do. We must be "determined to save / the only life [we can] save."[2]

So, how do we change, you ask? We do this with the help of my two good friends—patience and persistence. They have seen me through many difficult times. Though I am not naturally patient, I have learned to be more so. I am always pleased when I find myself behind a slow driver and I don't immediately start swearing and honking my horn. Instead, I use the moment as an opportunity to breathe and to reflect on the weather, my life, my blessings, or what to cook for dinner. Learning to be patient has brought out the poet in me. Sitting quietly in meditation, I see images, hear words flow. And even if I am not meditating, I am poised, patiently, for pictures to form in my brain. Patience is such a challenging practice. Everything in me wants to react rather than respond to life, but being patient pays off beautifully. Life is smoother, more serene. Peaceful.

At the same time, I have tempered my persistence so that I don't charge like a bull into a china shop at every turn. Having said that, I can think of at least ten times in the last month when I have forged ahead without consulting anyone, to get a job done. Usually the job falls flat. I always regret not having paused and asked someone what *they* think or what *they* might do, because if I have learned nothing else in my sixty-plus years on this planet, it is that we do not live in a vacuum. It is our responsibility to connect with others—or pay the consequences.

Recently, I had an idea that I thought was golden. I decided that my publisher and I should use my illustrator friend to design the cover of my new book. I went ahead and gave instructions to the artist about exactly what I thought the cover should look like. He took me at my word and produced exactly what I asked for. It was not what I imagined, which may seem ironic because the cover was *precisely* what I had imagined. But it just didn't fit. So, I ate the cost of paying him and left the design to real designers. My enthusiasm cost me—in time and in money. Rather than taking the time to discuss it with others, I acted on my idea because I thought it was the right thing to do. That should have been my first clue, those words "because I think." Who is it that said, "When I am in my mind, I am behind enemy lines?" Maybe not enemy lines, but definitely in need of a second opinion. Needless to say, my great idea did not pan out.

So, how do we make the transition to being more kind, more patient, less impulsive? For now, and from the very beginning of our transformation, we can pretend. We can pretend we are patient and tolerant. We can pretend we are loving and confident. I am actually not saying anything original. You have probably heard the phrase, "fake it 'til you make it." One of my favorite songs is from the musical *The King and I*. In it, the songwriter expresses the idea of "acting as if" as a way to overcome negative behavior. "Make believe you're brave ... / You may be as brave / as you make believe you are."[3]

Acting "as if" may seem fake at first, even a little dishonest, but how much better to act pleasant than to be, honestly, a pain in everyone's life? The beauty of this technique is that you never get it perfect, at least I never have. But that's not the point. The point is that you are making an effort to change your "bad" behavior to "good" behavior. The more you practice, the more success you will have with it.

I know I have had success with this practice, particularly at work. Occasionally, there will be someone at work who rubs me the wrong way. My immediate reaction will be to start picking them apart— their clothes, their weight, the way they talk and boss people around, the food they eat on break. Then, my better self tells me, "No. Put yourself in their shoes. Maybe they have a thyroid problem or cirrhosis of the liver. That's why their stomach is so large. Maybe they can't afford to eat anything but chips and white bread. Maybe they're insecure and so they feel like they need to tell everyone what to do." And so forth and so on. I act as if I am tolerant, compassionate, non-judgmental, until I actually feel some kindness toward the person. Magically, the barrier between us disappears. Mind you, they will never be my best friend, but I am no longer hard on them. Or on myself for being mean.

All of this talk of "good" and "bad" leads me to another thought. There really is no "good" or "bad," there just *is*. It is our perspective that makes things seem so. For example, take dust. Historically, dust has a bad rap. How many of you, when I mentioned the word "dust," thought of the phrase used at funerals (and derived from a verse in the book of Genesis), "ashes to ashes, dust to dust"? So often, death is the meaning attributed to dust. Dust can also be perceived as stagnation. Dust settles and accrues when nothing moves; it is not until we begin to make changes in our lives—both physical and spiritual—that the dust that has settled becomes animated, signifying transformation. This is a positive thing.

So, given that the dust will rise when we begin our transformation, and there will be debris we have to deal with, how do we stay the course? Here are some tools that have helped me on my journey:

TOOLKIT #1: CLEARING DUST

SURRENDER. One of the most iconic scenes in any movie ever made is in *The Wizard of Oz* when the Wicked Witch soars across the sky on her broomstick spelling out, "Surrender, Dorothy." Those words signify the end for poor Dorothy, as surrender often does. We hear that word—"surrender"—and we may think this (or we may not, depending on the scenario): loser, weakling, lost cause. "Surrender" is one of the most difficult tools to pick up because everything in us is taught to be a winner, a champion, a star. And yet, when we surrender, we actually align ourselves with a Universe that is profoundly abundant and loving. When we let go, our lives don't end. Instead, they begin a new and wonderful journey. The broomstick, the catalyst that made us surrender in the first place, becomes the broom that starts to clean up the debris on our side of the street.

Let go and let God. I remember the first time anyone told me to "let go and let God." I was standing in my parents' kitchen by the old white refrigerator, speaking on the beige phone that hung from the wall. (That's how phones were back in 1981, before cell phones that are now as slim as paper and contain your entire life.) I was terrified. I had been trying to stop drinking for two weeks since my first twelve-step meeting, and I couldn't. Even when I got rid of all the booze in the house, I still drank vanilla extract, cooking sherry, and mouthwash. I couldn't stop myself. I pleaded with my friend to tell me what to do.

"Turn it over," he told me. "Let go."

He might as well have told me to walk on the ceiling with my fingers crossed. Those words made no sense to me. I didn't understand what he meant by "turn it over." Turn what over? A piece of paper? My hands? The rug on the floor? And as for letting go, what was I to let go of? The whole idea was so foreign to me. In my world, if something was bothering you, you charged at it with a battering ram or bombed it with ten tons of dynamite. In my world, I was the solution to any problem. Now, suddenly, my friend was telling me that I actually was the problem. That I needed to step out of the way and let those who were better equipped handle it. I am not sure whether he said it in so many words, but the rest of his message came across as, "If you don't let go, if you don't surrender, you will never stop drinking and even if you don't die, you will only know misery."

I was ready to surrender.

Over the years, I have had to surrender again and again, in every area of my life. I have let go of resentments toward people and jobs, dreams and goals that were ego-driven, unreasonable demands on myself and others, self-centeredness, fear, superiority, depression, self-pity, unhealthy eating habits, self-flagellation, taking myself too seriously, not taking myself seriously enough, self-hatred, and much more.

Letting go is an ongoing process. In fact, every morning I turn my life and will over to the care of my Higher Power. As theologian and author C.S. Lewis said, "Relying on God has to begin all over again each day, as if nothing had yet been done." In the Old Testament, the Israelites who wandered in the desert were given enough manna for each day, no more. Surrender is like manna; it covers me for that twenty-four-hour period only. But it covers those twenty-four hours quite well.

Letting go is the spiritual wrench that loosens a soul that has been tightened to the extreme. But there are other little tools that are useful in clearing debris throughout the day. I have listed some of them below. The more you use these tools, the more your life will change. For some, the change seems to be immediate and volcanic. Many people say that even after just a few months, they feel like a different person. Let me caution you against this microwave transformation. It has been my experience that those who stay the course and truly live to *experience* a joy-filled life are those who take things slowly ... which is not to say you won't feel some immediate differences. You will. But the great spiritual leaders— like the Dalai Lama, Archbishop Desmond Tutu, and former President Jimmy Carter—didn't get where they are in one day. Take a lesson from plants that sprout from seed and then patiently grow before they burst into flower. Bloom where you are planted, and wait for that bloom to come. Be patient. And trust.

So, in all things, practice letting go. But be patient and persistent. As Aesop once wrote: "Slow and steady wins the race."

DON'T *BLAME* ANYONE. Not even yourself. Not anyone else. You are where you are, and you can move forward as long as you are not carrying a sack full of resentments and regrets. If you are an alcoholic or you suffer from a mental disorder, you are not to blame. You cannot help your genetics, but what you can do is to make good choices from here on out. Carrying regrets and blame is useless. All they do is weigh you down. And there is a difference between blaming yourself and taking responsibility for your actions. Sure, you have to look at your part in your relationships ... someday. Not today.

Do something nice for yourself and for someone else. Just a little thing. Maybe you make your partner their favorite dinner, or send your parents a thank-you card for just being who they are. For yourself, go to the library and borrow a book you have always wanted to read, or buy flowers, or a pair of boots. It doesn't have to be expensive. The simpler the better. It's just something to say, "I love you." Sound hokey? It's not. You will surrender more easily if you give yourself a hug than if you beat yourself with a stick.

Accept that the shit is going to hit the fan. There will be naysayers in your life who maybe aren't even naysayers, they are just skeptical (based on your past history) or afraid (wondering how your change is going to affect them). If you can accept that they have a right to feel exactly the way they feel about your decision to make that change, everyone will be happier. There is an old saying you might bear in mind: "What other people think about me is none of my business."

TREAD LIGHTLY. This applies not only to actions around others but toward yourself. Embarking on a program of self-transformation can be a heady endeavor, but don't let it go to your head! Remember: any journey is only as good as the steps you take. Walk lightly rather than stomping your way into a new self. You'll get there easier, though no faster. Time takes time.

FIND A BUDDY. Quickly. Someone you can vent to when the outside world is driving you crazy with comments and criticism. This might be an individual who you trust or a group. Anyone who can help you stay on course and listen when you just need to spew off. Then, find *another* buddy. This one an individual— one who has nothing invested in your remodeling— whose advice you respect and to whom you will listen for suggestions. Your other buddies can let you rant. This buddy will quiet you down and help you look at yourself so you can see the bigger picture.

BE STILL AND TRUST. As Julian of Norwich said, "All will be well. All will be well. All manner of things will be well." Transformation takes time. For everyone. You aren't the only one growing and changing. All that debris around you is changing too. But know this: while everything seems to be whirling around you, you don't have to whirl. Everything is working out just the way it is supposed to.

ACT "AS IF." Choose one area in your life that is the most troublesome and try surrendering that. Many people use driving as a place to start. When you are about to call the driver in front of you a nasty name, breathe in. When you exhale, send them good thoughts for a pleasant day. Do this with every jerk on the road and watch your stress level diminish.

LAUGH. Another valuable tool is laughter and not taking oneself too seriously. As someone with a dark side, I appreciate this the most. Someone asked me at a reading recently if I had learned anything in writing my last book. Without hesitation, I replied, "I found out I was funny!" I hadn't known that about myself for sixty-three years. That may be what drew me to my husband. He has the most irreverent sense of humor. Even as he faced life-threatening surgery, he was cracking jokes with the doctors. When he emerged from his transplant and insisted on doing laps around the intensive care unit, the doctors asked him if he was trying to show everybody up. To which he replied, "No, I'm just trying to fart." Laughter helps me accept the *shit* that is bound to happen. The weather. The dead battery. The broken zipper. And if I am not amused, I can practice another tool—I can act "as if."

> To have written a book that makes people laugh—
> and to laugh myself—is such a gift. One of the best
> benefits of clearing up debris is learning not to wear
> life like a lead mantle, but rather a loose garment.

In this chapter, we have started the process for our journey toward a happy, useful, and joy-filled life. Remodeling, as you can already tell, will not always be pretty, and it certainly won't be fast. For me, I have taken years to reveal and remove the debris caused by my active alcoholism and my bipolar disorder. These tools are not a "one and done" experience. We need to avail ourselves of them every day. If we do, we will move forward in our recovery, but remember it is "progress not perfection" that we seek.

When I surrendered my unmanageable life to the Universe, and asked for help, the process began to move forward like magic. Once I surrendered, I needed to let go and to trust in the goodness of my Creator. That didn't happen overnight, but little by little, I have let go of the illusion that I control things and have learned to hold on tighter to God's hand. One of the most valuable tools I learned early on that helped me grow closer to my Higher Power is that of self-love: I need to love myself, not blame myself or others, and be nice both to myself and the world around me. Such actions made me more available to be useful, which in turn gave me sorely lacking self-esteem.

༄

All these tools help me to cope with the plethora of bad feelings and thoughts I will undoubtedly have once I embark on my remodeling. It goes without saying that you will have times when you question your choice to stay sober or to stick to your medication, to make your doctor's appointments, and eat and exercise as you should. But if you practice with these tools listed above, you will be wearing better spiritual armor to keep you safe in the event of an ambush.

So, get busy! Pick up your tools! They are the tools that will help you create a life you can now only dream of.

CHAPTER 2
Set a Firm Foundation

Our town decided to construct a new shopping center in a vast, empty field that separates a little neighborhood from the highway. Appalled at first by yet another ravaging of land, I am somewhat amazed by what I see: all those giant machines straight off a Hollywood sci-fi set, complete with little men in lime-green vests.

The process began with moving enormous amounts of dirt off the site in big trucks and creating huge piles to the side of the highway, or *removing debris*. Next came leveling the field. Great care was taken to comb and recomb the land until it was flat. This stage actually took months, and not because the workers were lazy or inept. They tended the dirt carefully, raking and re-raking until they were satisfied. Then, hundreds of sticks with flags dotted the site. The concrete was poured and smoothed with huge blades like straight-edged razors as, slowly, the process evolved. Today, the stores have been built,

their foundations laid with utmost attention to detail. I
have great faith that the buildings are on firm footing.

Now what does this have to do with transforming
a life?

The foundation on which we build our lives dictates
the success, or failure, of our days. Like many men and
women born in 1950s America, I was brought up with a
Judeo-Christian foundation. My father, an officer in the
British Army, became an Episcopal priest after the war.
He went on to work in church schools in New England
and the mid-Atlantic. Needless to say, his family of six
daughters went with him.

I was attached to my father's hip as a young girl,
following him to chapel for early morning services,
Evensong every Wednesday, and Sunday services on the
weekend. Religion was a central part of my upbringing.
So, as a young child, I devoured books like *If Jesus Came
to My House* because, more than anything, I longed to
have Jesus as my friend.

Still, despite all the time I spent in church and all the
stories of Jesus' birth and his special place in Heaven, I
had my doubts. Not about God. I believed in God, but
I doubted that Jesus was who everyone told me he was.
To me, he just seemed like a really nice guy, *one* of God's
children, just like me.

I was as embarrassed and scared of having these
thoughts as I was of telling my mother I had started to
menstruate. What was wrong with me? Why couldn't
I just believe? I wanted to believe, but belief did not
come. Still, I persisted during my teens to serve on the
altar guild, to celebrate Christmas and Easter, and to

search through books, prayer, and meditation, for the key that would unlock my disbelief and make me true to the foundation of my youth. In my late twenties, when I had three years of sobriety and my focus was on my spiritual growth, I even went so far as to attend Yale Divinity School in the hope I would get definitive, persuasive answers to my questions.

All I got was confused.

I remember preaching as a young seminarian on All Saints Day, delivering the message that "We are all saints." I was certain I would be struck by lightning as I stood at the pulpit, feeling very much the fraud for delivering such a blasphemous message. But I believed then, and I still do, that we *are* all saints. Or can be. I think Jesus was a special prophet, one of God's chosen, along with Gandhi and Martin Luther King Jr., the Dalai Lama, Archbishop Tutu, and Jimmy Carter. When I left divinity school, my foundation was deeply shaken. Frankly, I was lost.

Here, a twelve-step program came to my rescue. The program never says we have to believe in any specific religion, or any religion at all. What it says is we need to come to believe in a power greater than ourselves. That can be anything. It might be Christianity, with Jesus Christ as your Savior, or it might not be. You might choose to turn to Buddhist teachings or the Koran. To Nature. To Judaism, Hinduism, Zoroastrianism. Maybe you turn to physics or another field of science. Or maybe you just turn to the members of your recovery group. "GOD" for you may simply be "Good Orderly Direction" or a "Group of Drunks."

Arlo Guthrie said it best as he related a story on a podcast my husband and I listened to. He spoke of returning to the location of "Alice's Restaurant," which, as you may recall, was located on the second floor of a church. A pastor came along, knocked on the glass doors and asked Arlo, "Hey, what kind of church is this?" To which Arlo responded, "The 'Bring Your Own God' variety." A worthy answer, in my mind.[4]

The point is, you turn somewhere, you come to believe in something, and you then begin to trust. Trust is, I believe, the firmest foundation we can have for building a new life. For me, the moment I began to trust in a power outside myself was the moment my journey toward a new, purposeful life began.

It would be misleading to suggest that my trust began when I put down alcohol and drugs though. It did not. My relationship with a power greater than myself had begun long before that, when I was about twelve years old. At that time, I made the decision to place my trust in something other than the Church, and turned to nature. While the woods were a lovely refuge, they were not the substitute "power" I was looking for. However, it was there in the woods that I met Mr. Riley.

Mr. Riley was not a human being. He was a voice I heard both in my head and my heart. He counseled me when I was grieving and gave me courage when I was afraid. Some people would call him an imaginary friend, but to me he was quite real and quite comforting. Above all, he was trustworthy. When I prayed to Mr. Riley, he heard my cries and he answered.

I remember clearly one day in my early teens when I called on Mr. Riley for help. I was volunteering at the Baltimore Museum of Art. It was a Sunday afternoon, and I wanted to say goodbye to a boy who had stayed at our house over the weekend to attend a school dance. We often hosted visiting boys because we had so much room in our house, and this boy was in town as another girl's date. The girl was a friend of my sister's, but that didn't stop me from flirting with her beau. I had fallen head over heels for him even though he was five years older than I was. So, I wanted, needed, to see him one last time before he left.

I sat in the far back of the beige station wagon on the way home from the art museum, trying to stifle my sobs so my sister and the other girls who had volunteered at the museum that day would not tease me. The seat faced backwards and I stared at the cars coming up behind us. I could feel George, the gentle black man who was driving, looking at me in the rearview mirror as I wept and wailed and prayed with all the intensity of a lovesick teen. How could Greg have left and gone back to Mercersburg without one more smile? I prayed to Mr. Riley to intervene.

My schoolmates and sister in the station wagon were pragmatic. They reasoned that the handful of boys who had made the trek to our all girls' school had probably returned to their school already. After all, it was a long drive back to Pennsylvania. There would be no chance those boys were waiting on us to get home. But those same girls jumped on my prayer wagon, closed their eyes, and held hands, praying aloud to Mr. Riley that Greg would wait for us. George did his part by exceeding the speed limit and, when the traffic mounted, we prayed harder. We never gave up until the moment we drove into the school and saw Greg and his schoolmates leaning against their van, waiting to take the long ride back to their dormitories in Pennsylvania, oblivious to all our supplications.

Right then and there my trust was solidified.

I have had so many similar "coincidences" in my life. And not just the obvious ones, like having tax returns come just on time or finding the perfect curtains on sale. My trust in my Higher Power, whom I no longer call Mr. Riley, is based on deeper circumstances.

જ

Years later, in 1978, when I was twenty-three years old and in the throes of alcoholism, I cried out, "Help!" I don't know why on that random day the supplication was so sincere. I guess I was just "sick and tired of being sick and tired." I did not know who I was calling to. I had long since given up on a belief in Mr. Riley. I just knew I could not go on the way things were for one minute more. I blamed my irritability, my misery, my discontent on my then-husband. If only he had been different. If only he had been Tom Selleck, *Magnum P.I.* If only he didn't drink the way he did, if only he paid more attention to me. If only I had been a bestselling author, rich and famous, my life would have been fabulous.

In truth, that was my alcoholism speaking. I just didn't know it. I didn't know my problems were not external, they were internal. I felt helpless, hopeless. I had alienated my family, my friends. I had nowhere to turn, but I needed help desperately. I believe now that God heard me in that moment of desperation and graced me with his presence in my life. Though I didn't realize it at the time, things began to change as soon as I said, "Help!"

In retrospect, everything seems so clear to me. Not long after my "breakdown," I read about the Bennington Writer's Workshop in Vermont; I applied, and I went. Over drinks and conversation, I ingratiated myself to George Garrett, the director of the program. I was the same old me, full of arrogance and ego. Still, George seemed to think I had promise as a writer and asked me to TA for him at the Stone Coast Writers' conference in Maine the following summer.

There was never anything sexual with George. He was just a very nice man, kind, who smiled a lot and laughed. But sex did rear its head. One of the women enrolled in the Bennington program had brought her sixteen-year-old son with her. The boy was sweet and good-looking, and the two of us talked a lot and played tennis together. In my mind, I was his "Mrs. Robinson," although I was only seven years his senior, and it was my job to initiate him to the world of sex. So, one hot August afternoon, we locked the door to my small dorm room, stripped, and made love. I felt so proud, as though I had given him a great gift. In truth, I guess that "gift" would have been considered illegal in most states. That's just where my head was though—grandiose. Self-centered. What if that boy had regretted sleeping with me when he found the girl of his dreams?

The next year, in August of 1981, when I was nearly twenty-five years old, I took off from Boston in my Volvo station wagon, which was filled to the brim with bottled water. I had made the firm resolve that I would not drink alcohol at this conference—despite my anxiety that I was going to fail, that I was no good, that George had made a mistake. Within minutes of arriving in Maine, the director of the conference asked me if I would like to go for beer. Without hesitation, I was off and running. My drinking took off to a new level, and my behavior followed. One night, some of the guest authors and participants and I piled into my Volvo to go bar hopping in Portland. I was the designated driver, by choice, but I could not keep myself from drinking. I remember driving back to the campus that night, half in the bag, with at least one poet laureate in my car, thinking, "I am going to kill these people." I could not see, all I could do was pray that God would get us safely back or hope the police would pull me over. At that moment, I swore I would stop drinking forever.

Of course, as soon as we arrived safely, I took back my promise and hit the wine. After that ordeal, didn't I deserve a drink? I certainly needed one.

The week progressed. To make up for the inadequacies I felt as a writer, I slept with anyone and everyone who showed up at my door. One night, the poet laureate came to my room, where I lay half-drunk on my bed. We had sex and I felt special. Here was a famous poet who wanted to have sex with me. But the night turned uglier when the director of the conference appeared at my door, insisting I put out for him too. We argued. I didn't want to. But in the end, I gave in because I didn't know how to say no. Not to booze. Not to sex either.

One man I *did* want to have sex with was a handsome, blond writer from California. There was something about him that was different from all the other men at the conference. For one thing, he wasn't hitting on me, which made him all the more desirable. I pursued him relentlessly, pounding on his door at night when I was drunk. He didn't answer. Didn't say anything. He would just wait until day, then talk with me about a book I was writing and how I could be the next great thing.

One afternoon, he came to my room and found me there, passed out and surrounded by wine bottles. He told me I might benefit from a twelve-step program. I didn't know what that meant, but I told him I would go if he would sleep with me.

ॐ

That first twelve-step group meeting was just what I had expected it would be, if I had gone with any expectations. In truth, I didn't know what to expect. It was a bunch of old men wearing trench coats and smoking cigarettes in front of the American flag. I felt so out of place and even angry that my friend had thought this was where I belonged. The whole program turned me off, but the seed was planted. I had heard enough to know there was something out there for me, some hope. My friend never did plant *his* seed in me, but we kept in touch over the next few weeks.

I was housesitting for my parents in Vermont and trying desperately to stop drinking, but I couldn't stop. I lied to my friend and told him I was fine. Even when there was no booze in the house, I would chug mouthwash, cooking sherry, vanilla extract, *anything* to try to get a buzz. Finally, I got honest with him and told him what was going on. He told me what to do: pray. Don't drink. Go to a meeting. Even with all my difficulties, I could not bring myself to go to a meeting in my parents' hometown in Vermont. I was afraid of what people would say about them, their daughter an alcoholic and Dad a parish priest! (Ironically, when I *did* start going to meetings in Bennington, members of the group there told me they had been saving a seat for my father for many years.) So, I white-knuckled my sobriety until I returned to Boston. Then, when I finally found a meeting that seemed like one I would like, I went. Mt. Auburn Hospital, Sunday night, September 14, 1981.

I have stayed sober continuously since.

I now know my Higher Power was working for me at that time. I'd received help when I needed it because when I'd cried out, deep down, I was desperate for my prayers to be answered.

☞

Desperation is a critical element in laying a firm foundation. Without desperation, we believe we can handle everything, and that we *are* handling everything. In fact, we are keeping a working faith at arm's distance.

When I was still drinking excessively, I lived under the misconception that *I* was making my life happen. And, in one way, I was. I was responsible for the failed jobs, the ruined relationships, the squandered funds, the poor health. I didn't know then, or even imagined, there could be a life that was much more enjoyable, free of worries, and based on honesty, compassion, and love. I had read about that kind of life, but I had long since lost the hope of such a change for me … until I got sober and began to seek a God of my understanding. The God I needed was not your God, not my father's God, not the God of Elie Wiesel or Mahatma Gandhi. I needed to find *my* God, the God who made *my* bones and who filled *my* heart with joy. The God who spoke to me, personally. A God in whom I could trust.

Seeking God for me has been less an intellectual exercise and more like a childhood game. I wake every morning with my hands over my eyes—peek-a-boo!— ready for the fun to begin. As I walk through my day, I hear, see, and feel God in so many things. My God doesn't sit like a judge in the pages of a book. My God is in the clouds and the birds, in messages on church bulletin boards, on my digital clock and on license plates, in tea kettles and tax returns, traffic and parking spaces, lanes in the pool, morning meditations, sales on dresses, and in hand-me-downs, strangers, neighbors, and dogs. I seek God in everything.

I see God in every *thing*.

I have since early sobriety, but especially since I had my own spiritual awakening at the time of my husband's rebirth.

For example, one morning recently, as I was driving back from the gym with my husband, I was troubled and expressing my anxiety to him. Intellectually, I knew better than to worry about the things that were eating me up—my part-time job, a woman I sponsor, silence from publishers (the list goes on). As we drove past the local Catholic Church, I noticed the banner they had posted on their digital board: PRAY HOPE, DON'T WORRY. It seemed to have been written just for me! ... Of course, what it really said was PRAY, HOPE, DON'T WORRY, but I liked what I saw.

Please don't misunderstand me. My trust in God is not based on fortune cookies and palmistry. Much of my trust stems from the passion and conviction of the Psalms. My favorite, Psalm 139, verses 7-12, describes my relationship with the God of my understanding:

Whither shall I go from thy spirit? or whither shall I flee from thy presence? If I ascend up into heaven, thou art there: if I make my bed in Sheol, thou art there. If I take the wings of the morning, and dwell in the uttermost parts of the sea; Even there shall thy hand lead me, and thy right hand shall hold me. If I say, 'Let only darkness cover me, and the light about me be night,'even the darkness is not night to thee; the night is as bright as the day; for darkness is as light to thee. (The New Oxford Annotated Bible)

ॐ

God knows me, has always known me, but do I know God? There is a saying, "If God is missing from my life, who moved?" Laying a firm foundation means to continually, actively, constantly seek God's presence in my life. For me, the God of my understanding has manifested Himself as Love. My God is bigger than all religions, does not exclude anyone, sees the good in all things, cares deeply about all creation, delights in creating, weeps at destruction, and makes all things possible. Your God may be entirely different from mine; you may not even call what you trust "God." But in order to lay a firm foundation for life, we have to trust in *something* outside ourselves.

I have heard people in the program say, "Oh, you can believe in *anything* if you are not ready to take the leap. Believe in that fire hydrant or your monster truck. They can be your Higher Power for now." To that I say, "Bullshit." Perhaps the fire hydrant was conveniently placed and enabled the fire department to put out the fire in your home before your house burned down. And maybe that made the hydrant seem like a *gift* from God. But it is not *God*.

Don't waste your time and effort stalling. Take the leap. Let yourself imagine for five minutes that there is something in the Universe that cares for you deeply, that has your best interests at heart, that wants you to be happy, joyous, and free.

My experience has been if I even open up my heart to the improbability of such Love, my Higher Power will swoop in and make things right, in both small and not so small ways.

༈

Fast forward to 2015. One night, several months after my husband's liver transplant, he went into rejection. We rushed him to the hospital in Charlotte where they were waiting to determine what had gone wrong with the surgery. When we arrived at the hospital, a sign by the parking garage read LOT FULL. The attendant waved us on but I convinced him to let us in. Despite his mutterings that there were no spots to be found, I turned to Thom and said, "Just wait and see what God is going to do now." We had no further gone up the ramp and turned the bend when a white car drove toward us, leaving an open spot behind. The license plate on the car read "GOD."

You just can't make this stuff up.

I've given up trying to remember how many of these instances have occurred in the past thirty-eight years. My kids laugh and call me "lucky." I *am* lucky, but not because little miracles happen all the time. I am lucky because I have a firm foundation of trust in my Higher Power, which makes everyday living an absolute joy. Imagine no longer having to worry about anything, but trusting that everything is just as it is supposed to be. Imagine not stressing out about money, love, children, health or food because you trust enough to let the Universe help you with those problems. This is not about sitting back in your armchair and letting the world spin, by the way. Trust is a very active thing.

ॐ

One of the big things I have had to learn and practice is *how* to Trust. I have to trust myself at the same time I have to watch myself. The other day, I asked a friend why she had taken a specific action. She told me, "God told me to." While God may have spoken to her in previous incidences, in this case I told her she was full of shit. God had no more told her than I had feathers. It was her ego that led to her choice. That's why we have friends, so that when we are unable to see ourselves as we truly are, others can watch for us.

For my part, I find that if I am listening to stuff in my head that is untrustworthy and suspect, I get angry and morose. If I listen to messages of rationalization and justification, my throat gets dry and my face reddens. After years of getting to know myself better, I have learned what it takes to keep my trust in myself and to therefore be trustworthy for others. My well-being is like a three-legged stool: take my medication daily, as prescribed; be honest with myself and others; rely on the God of my understanding. This leads to a hopeful, joyous, stable frame of mind.

When I depend upon the three legs of the stool to guide my actions, I trust, and because I trust, I can write my books and send them out to publishers. I trust, so I have faith that when I need clothes, someone will give me hand-me-downs. I trust that the right person, the right message will come to me at exactly the right time. Because I trust, it's easy to assume the world is going to take care of me. But I need to bring the shovel and do the work.

Part of the work of trusting is being open to unforeseen outcomes. If we hold on to our old expectations, we don't allow the Universe to surprise us (possibly with something we never even imagined). For me, the best way to be open to what my Higher Power has in store is to stay within a very quiet routine of exercise, eating right, sleeping, writing, and meetings.

Nothing I am telling you is new. There are hundreds of books that say the same thing, or similar, but the difference is, what *I* am saying is not just a theory. I didn't read this in some magazine or journal and try to apply it to my life. This is not about statistics and fads, bestsellers and moneymakers. This *is* my life. It is a life that has changed radically from one of fear, worry, and doubt to a life of joy, hope, and possibility. It is also a life that I have earned, in part, from working very hard at being truthful, trustful, trustworthy.

No foundation of trust can be built without honesty. If you cannot, will not, be honest with yourself, you will have a very hard time staying on the path of recovery. Self-delusion will drag you into the bushes and steal your ID, your money, and your phone. And you may not remember, when you come to, just who you are. So, I have always, always, always made it a point to tell on myself. Ask anyone who knows me. I talk. A lot. I humble myself. I *embarrass* myself. Sometimes I embarrass others. Who likes to admit they shoplifted and had to return the item to the manager?

Who takes pride in having to return change that doesn't belong to them? Who enjoys telling their spouse they spent money they shouldn't have, on things they didn't need? Most folks don't, and they rationalize to avoid it.

Rationalization creates a slippery slope away from trust. If you are rationalizing your poor behavior on the one hand and, on the other hand, having expectations that others should behave a certain way, you are, as they say, "stuck between a rock and a hard place." Odysseus lost a few men there. Don't you fall victim too.

~

In order to have a secure house, you need a firm foundation. A firm foundation in human terms does not necessarily imply a religious connection, though that may exist. It suggests a *trusting* relationship with something outside ourselves. When we enjoy that relationship, life becomes full of miracles.

Beware the traps of expectation and rationalization that bar the way to joy!

TOOLKIT #2

TRUST is the WD-40 lubricant of our spiritual toolkit. It greases the connections we make to our Higher Power, opening the door to the Divine. Even if the door is opened only a crack, God will take the initiative and enter our lives. What steps can those of us for whom a lack of trust has been the status quo take to move toward willingness? And for those who have never known trust at all, what does that trust even look like? Here are some suggestions that I offer as a way of developing trust—in God, in ourselves, and in others. When you use these tools, you will see positive changes—sometimes quickly, sometimes slowly—in your ability to trust.

MAKE YOUR BED AND HIT YOUR KNEES. Books have been written on the value of making your bed every day. I can't say I buy all the theories, but I do encourage the practice. For me, making my bed every day is the first step I take in assuring myself that I am committed to my own self-care. When I smooth the sheets and pull up the covers, I am setting my intention for a smooth day. I am also renewing my personal trustworthiness. I can count on myself to keep a promise I made to *me* to start each day with a tidy bed, a bed that will be inviting at the end of the day.

While I am making my bed, tucking sheets and blankets, I sometimes (less often now that I am older and my knees have issues) fall to my knees, close my eyes, and thank the Universe for granting me the gift of another day. Whether I am kneeling, standing, or sitting, I can count on myself to express this gratitude. I do it every day, wherever I am. Some might ask, "Doesn't it just become rote? Like, you don't even mean it anymore?" My reply: "Is it boring to breathe? Is it boring to hear the birds sing at dawn?" Repetition doesn't necessitate boredom. What brings on boredom is lack of attention.

BE MINDFUL. Being mindful—paying attention—is one of the most effective ways to grow in trust with a Higher Power. Stilling the mind and just being where we are is often a mind-blowing experience! When I sit in our backyard and listen to the birds, I am stunned by the layers of song when previously I had assumed there was just one. As I walk on the lawn, I notice a myriad of flowers—tiny yellow buttercups, purple and white violets, lavender ajuga, minute white stars. Before, it just all looked green. Imagine if we were all to notice the variety of trees lining our neighborhood streets, not just the pink and white dogwoods and purple redbuds but *all* the greens, every shade from sage to hunter. Imagine if every minute we looked with the same awe and wonder at all creation? At our fellow man? When I walk, surrounded by all this beauty, I think about the creative impulse underlying all creation. I trust in the Divine impulse to create. I trust I am a part of that impulse, and my job, in God's image, is to be creative too.

KEEP YOUR PROMISES. It's all very well to be airy fairy about trust, but real trust is an almost tangible thing. Perhaps I trust you because you are trustworthy. Or you show up when you say you are going to show up. You charge me what you say you are going to charge me. You keep your promises. I can count on you to be reliable, punctual, and true. Very little gets under my skin more than someone who is not punctual, so I learned long ago to set a fifteen-minute rule. If you are not at the place you said you would be within fifteen minutes of our agreed time, I feel justified to walk away. That way, I haven't wasted my day and I can leave without resentment. Of course, if you have called with extenuating circumstances, that is different. The rule is a common courtesy that respects everyone's time.

BELIEVE IN YOURSELF. A big part of trusting God and others is learning to trust yourself. Frequently, people get in trouble in this area because they have made unreasonable demands on themselves. For example, at times in my life I have wanted to lose weight so I have gone on extreme, unrealistic, diets. Within days I have fallen off the wagon and gained even more weight back. What I had to do was find a sensible program that allowed me to eat all the foods I liked, just in smaller quantities, and encouraged me to give myself several months to take off the weight. Not weeks. This rational approach to eating allowed me to develop a whole new relationship with food. It also enabled me to build trust in myself that I could make healthy choices about my meals. As I make healthy, trustworthy choices, my self-esteem increases and I find I am even more eager to take care of myself.

ASK FOR HELP. Have you ever played the game "Trust" where you close your eyes and fall into someone's arms before you hit the ground? That one was always difficult for me, controlling as I was. Even more difficult for me was the notion of asking anyone for help. First, there was the issue of looking like a failure. If I asked for help, wasn't that an admission that I didn't know something, or couldn't handle it myself? And if I couldn't do everything perfectly, then did I really have a right to exist? I know that sounds extreme, but that is how I lived for many years. In practicing the twelve steps, I learned how my perfectionism was not the asset I had thought it to be. In fact, my perfectionism was possibly my greatest liability because it kept me apart from God and my fellows. I thought if I did so great—won all the English and drama awards at high school graduation, and several at college, looked good, etcetera—everyone would love me. On the contrary, they were turned off by my conceit and superiority.

This thinking reminds me of when I was about six years old. When we would leave the apartment, I would make my sisters turn out all the lights so the robbers would know we were not there and choose that moment to commit their crimes. That way, they wouldn't be tempted to come in and kill us when we actually *were* there. I think that is called "bass-ackward" thinking. When I attempted to win love and approval through my accomplishments and pride, I engaged in much the same process.

CHAPTER 3
Let Light In

We live in a brick ranch that still has its original 1960s floor plan. There are three reasonably-sized bedrooms, two modest full baths, a smallish kitchen, a good-sized living room, and a den. Nothing fancy or out of the ordinary ... except for the attached garage that is no longer a garage. That space is now a "bonus room" with a laundry at one end, and it's where my son lives with his computer and cat.

The room is dark. It's dreary. The fluorescent lights in the ceiling do not lend charm. For many years, I have entertained the idea of blasting through the back wall and installing a bay window that would look out on the gardens and pool. I've dreamed of dropping two skylights in the ceiling so he can see the stars, and so sunlight can pour into the room and lift it up from its heaviness, if such a thing is possible.

Light is magical. It cures so many ills. Medical doctors claim that a dose of vitamin D from the sun can help stave off both the common cold and depression alike. There are so many ways to lighten a life, so many lives that need brightening. I know mine did.

ॐ

I seem to have been born with a proclivity for darkness and fear. I am not talking about fear of monsters under the bed, though that was an issue, or breaking my mother's back by walking on the cracks. Nor am I referring to the fear that plagued me as a child when I contemplated the vastness of the Universe, not understanding how it could begin or end. What I mean is I was born with a very deep, pernicious fear that my parents were going to abandon me, that they didn't love me. What resulted was almost pathological behavior on my part. I would not let my father out of my sight.

In the morning, when he would go to fill the milk jugs at the refectory, I would accompany him, gripping his hand as if it were the very spark of life. To me, it was. I would travel with him every Sunday, not only to the first services he would do at the private school where we lived but also to his secondary parish miles away. When he and my mother went out to parties, I would make a scene until they agreed to let me go with them. If they had guests in the evening, I would sneak out of bed in my pajamas and end up dancing on my father's feet. All I wanted was to be near him, to make sure he never left me alone. Of course, we had to part ways when I went to school or he to his job, but at night, after everyone had gone to bed, I would sneak back into my parents' room and crawl in bed beside him. I believe at the root of my behavior was a fundamental fear that I would be, that I *was,* alone in the Universe. All my father's talk about God couldn't diminish the desolation I felt inside.

At an early age, I started to question and to analyze existence. I read for deeper meanings in books that other children just read for fun. A favorite book from my childhood, *Michael Grows a Wish,* is about a young boy (Michael) who wants a horse. He works very hard to take care of an old sawhorse his father has given to him, proving that Michael is both responsible and dedicated to his dream. On his birthday, he walks into the stable and there in the stall is a real horse! He is ecstatic, even though the horse is fat and mangy. He treats her like a queen. Then one day, his queen plops down and births a foal. Beautiful, black, and sleek, the colt is just what Michael has been hoping for. When I read that story as a young child, I immediately understood that if I worked hard, persisted, and believed, I could make all my dreams come true, without any help from parents or others. Thus began the slippery slope to isolation and to the skewed thinking which told me I had to achieve in order to be of value.

The trouble with my alcoholism and bipolar disorder is that, dormant or active, they made the *possibility* or *desire* to work hard and achieve goals a *necessity.* I lost the option to fantasize, to imagine my dreams coming true. Very gradually, my understanding of life became skewed, and I was held captive by unrelenting and unrealistic imaginings of what my life was, who I was, and what I was capable of achieving.

The trouble with believing you *must* do it all yourself is that life can become very bleak. Mine did. Through constantly pushing to achieve my goals, I alienated myself from family and friends. I am pretty sure my sisters despised me for my successes, and I didn't have any close confidants. My only companions in high school and college were those whom I met when I was in plays (acting was something I was very good at) ... or drinking. Because by the time I was a sophomore in high school, I was drinking on a regular basis to numb the feelings of anxiety and depression I harbored inside.

At that time in my life, I lived like a double agent. The overarching sense that I could—and must—succeed at everything I attempted was countered by a deepening sense of despair and anxiety that led me to believe I was capable of nothing. Like being stuck in fast-flowing water and trying to swim upstream, I went nowhere. I went backwards, if anywhere, as I sank further and further into my diseases.

The hardest thing about this period of my life was my inability, and the inability of those around me, to accept that I had a problem. It was one thing for my oldest sister to get pregnant in college (that was visible), or for my next oldest sister to join a commune and run away from home (that was an action). But I was standing with one foot in the territory of success and achievement while the other slipped over Death's threshold, and ... who knew? I was falling fast, but my parents had so many issues of their own, they hardly noticed my issues; even I wasn't convinced that there was a problem. Only one sister believed I had a problem, and hers was a small voice crying in the wilderness. And so, I persisted under the illusion that "I had it all under control."

～

During the Christmas vacation when I was a junior in high school, my family had gone to Vermont to be with friends over the New Year holiday. I had opted to stay at home, hoping my boyfriend would invite himself over for the night. He did not. So, I lit a fire in the giant fireplace in our living room, retrieved my parents' gallon jug of red wine from the pantry, and lay in front of the fire, drinking and listening to sad music. I felt wonderfully melancholy and artistic. I thought to myself, *This would make a wonderful scene in a movie.*

All the movies I watched were dark. Ingmar Bergman. Fellini. I prided myself on being an "artist" who watched deep foreign films, read Kierkegaard, and owned only one pair of jeans. Doom and gloom, intensity and darkness. I see these sentiments returning in society today, but this time with violence and hate. Being caught in negative feelings was like having glue on my feet. As long as I was caught there, I could do nothing else. Once I asked for help, on my knees, in my living room, new light began to shine in my life.

～

Let's talk some more about light. One of the most beloved songs in the popular movie *The Sound of Music* is "My Favorite Things." Even just thinking of that song brings a smile to my face, lets light into my soul. As a child, I already knew the transformative aspect of thinking about and engaging in those things we love. Today, we hear all about gratitude, and gratitude is an important practice. Back when I was young, I thought of this practice as following my Bliss.

It was Bliss that brought me to the stables at the boarding school where we lived to lie in the loft amidst the rectangular bales, smelling the sweet thickness of horses, sweet feed, and hay. It was Bliss that led me into the woods behind the horse barn to sit on a log over the brook, reading Robert Frost's poetry and watching the sunlight filter through the trees. Bliss prompted me to paint the furniture in my bedroom bright orange and yellow and to lacquer collages to anything in our home that had legs (excluding people and animals). Bliss encouraged me to play loud music, like "Suite: Judy Blue Eyes," and jog in my room (much to the dismay of my father whose study was just below me). It was my quest for Bliss that had me sunbathe nude on the fire escape landing outside my window and bake loaves of warm, brown bread to eat with butter and strawberry jam. Bliss brought me into lakes to swim and gave me a Siamese cat to love. Bliss laughed with me as I ran in the fields, gulping in Life, which at times when I was young seemed so often full of darkness. Bliss had me fall in love with a ginger boy during my junior year in high school.

Falling in love may seem like a positive thing, and to most people it is. But to me—untrained in relationships and suffering as I was from undiagnosed bipolar disorder—love was a disaster. What began as a flame quickly escalated into a wild fire, leaving behind a lot of collateral damage.

Looking back, I should have seen the end coming long before it did. He sent me lyrics to Bonnie Raitt songs with lines like, "If you don't love her, you'd better let her go." He didn't keep promises to me, never called and only seemed interested in getting me in trouble, but I was determined, by God, to hold on like a cowboy on a bucking horse. I would not let go easily.

Once, I let him hold a burning match to my hand and let it burn, until it blistered, to prove that I was impervious to any pain he could inflict. He seemed the perfect love for me, though where I got that idea, I have no clue. He was selfish and vain and aloof.

I see now that the way I clung to my boyfriend was just the way I clung to my father. And for the same reason: fear of not being loved.

჻

What is it about love that when you have it, you feel like a million bucks, but when it is taken away, you are left a pauper? I don't know if it was my bipolar disorder that made my boyfriend's rejection (after we had been together for several years) hit me so hard, but for the next eight years, I experienced little joy in my life. I coped with that monumental casting aside by pouring booze, sex, food, and drugs into my life. It took me a long time to climb out of that dark hole, for light to shine in my life again.

꒰

In the beginning of my transformation in the twelve-step program, and even still to this day, I was cautious. I was not looking for some glaring, billion-watt moment of enlightenment. I have always been more persuaded and encouraged by the small moments of grace that gently illuminate my day. The first such moment in recovery happened when I was about eighteen months into my sobriety. By then, I had divorced my ex-husband; landed a humbling, clerical job; moved into a rent-controlled apartment; and made new friends. Life was rolling along, almost too comfortably.

I needed a vacation. I needed a change. The problem was, I had no money. A friend who was into Shakti Gawain and creative visualization suggested I ask the Universe to send me on a trip. *Horse feathers,* I thought, and asked anyway. Within days, another friend said her parents were going to Barbados and all I had to do was come up with $432.87 for my part. I didn't have the money and cursed the Universe for toying with me. Literally, the next day, my tax return came back. Guess how much it was for? $432.87.

I know I have said it before, but it bears repeating: you can't make this stuff up.

꒰

Lighting up my life hasn't been just about getting what I wanted—though there has been plenty of that—it has been about *giving*. Giving is a huge part of bringing light into your life. But a word of caution: you must give to *give,* not give to get. For example, when my daughter and I sponsor families at Christmas time, as we have for many years, we don't do it because of what people will say or think—"Aren't they nice to do that?" "Isn't that just so kind?" We do it because we can imagine the children on Christmas day, opening presents they only dreamed of receiving. The pure, unadulterated happiness that comes from believing Santa is real. Last year my husband joined in. He picked out a Spider-Man bike for a little boy. It was a beautiful bike with all the bells and whistles, streamers and spokes. I wish I could have seen that child's face when he realized the bike was for him. But it's better I didn't. Just give to give. It definitely sparks an interior glow.

Sometimes giving is not as obvious. In the bookstore where I worked, I would once in a while come across a person who was off-putting at first. But if I gave them my attention and sincerely desired to help them solve their problem, suddenly we both softened, and when we parted there were handshakes and smiles. Sometimes even a hug. Being with people—whether strangers or loved ones—without judgement, with pure interest and love, is one of the best ways I know to light up my life.

Giving selflessly to others is a fundamental precept in many of the world's greatest religions and is at the root of the twelve-step program. The twelfth step of Alcoholics Anonymous stresses the necessity for the recovering alcoholic or addict to share the message of recovery with fellow sufferers in order to maintain their sobriety. Personally, I have found that working with those who are skeptical and afraid has enriched my own sobriety immensely and helped me to stay on course. There are so many paradoxes in the twelve-step program. That we cannot stay sober unless we serve other alcoholics is a vital one, and one that makes my life brighter every time I engage in a selfless act.

సా

None of this lighting up would be possible without my medication. I know there are differing opinions about the use of prescription drugs, especially in twelve-step programs. Some hardliners believe we should go commando and never put a pill in our bodies, that God will do the rest. These naysayers scare newcomers, who could benefit greatly from being on prescription medication, into thinking that a person is weak or flawed if they take what the doctor ordered. These zealots even go so far as to say that if you are on prescription medication, you are not sober. To that I cry, "Bullshit!" And I say, "Bullshit!" again to those who argue that everything can be cured holistically with the proper blend of kale, Greek yogurt, and beets. Don't get me wrong, I love a good smoothie and eating healthy is part of my routine, but using smoothies to calm a troubled mind is like fighting fire with gas. Expect an explosion.

I have been on medication for decades, and sometimes it was the *wrong* medication. In the early '90s, after my mother was killed in a head-on collision, I fell into a deep darkness that morphed into postpartum depression. Or so I was told. I was diagnosed by a rather incompetent doctor, who later disappeared without a word. He put me on fluoxetine (commonly known as Prozac), and there I stayed for the next few years, during my next pregnancy, getting worse and worse.

There is nothing more frightening and frustrating than being on a medication you are told should bring you relief but doesn't. The way I can best describe that feeling is as if you are hanging on to a rope, dangling over a deep pit full of hungry tigers, and your hands keep slipping. The more anxious you become, the more your palms sweat, the closer you are to the tigers—and certain death. That's what it was like with me on Prozac: I was trying to do what was right, to do what I was told, but the monsters kept chasing me, getting closer and closer. I finally erupted into mania at my father's funeral, and I was introduced, by the grace of God, to a skilled psychiatrist who saw my illness for what it was, diagnosed me with bipolar disorder, and worked with me over time to come up with a cocktail of pills that has enabled me to live a productive life, despite my mental illness.

I can't imagine living without my daily dose of lithium* and risperidone. My quality of life—the quality of life I share with my family and friends—is so positive and enjoyable because I take my medication. Without my meds, I would be a "crazy person" all over again. (Truth be told, I would probably be dead.) Taking my medication regularly, consistently, is probably the single most important thing I do to let light into my life. Am I ashamed of my reliance on prescriptions? Not at all! I would be foolish not to use them. What shame can

* See Author's Note at end of book.

there be in using a tool that God has given me to stay healthy, hopeful, humble? My husband wouldn't think of going without his tacrolimus, a necessity since his liver transplant. Why would I even consider foregoing the very thing that allows joy to enter my life?

჻

While medication can help to keep those of us who need it mentally healthy, equally as important is fresh air and exercise. There is a saying, "Move a muscle, change a mood." I can't tell you how many times I have been sitting on the couch, feeling lethargic and kind of glum, and I have pulled myself up and out for a walk, a swim, yoga, or even just a stroll in the backyard to check on what is blooming. Simply moving clears away the crap that has settled in my head. Of course, doctors will tell you all about the magic of endorphins, and I believe them, but I don't need to know this to feel motivated. It is enough for me to know that when I engage in something physical, my outlook shifts, and light breaks through.

Let me share one of my own poems with you:

LYE BROOK FALLS, VERMONT

You walk a rocky path,
careful not to twist an ankle,
stumble, fall.
The stones, tripping you up,
like character flaws,
remind you to be patient,
mindful.
Your legs burn,
your thighs are on fire.
Your heart throbs inside your chest,
every beat felt,
resonating through your body
to your brain.
You bump your head, curse
the low branches and fallen trees
that arch over the path.
You traverse streams,
over slippery stones,
telling yourself you will fall.
Don't fall.
You've got this.
Your sneakers get soggy,
your toes turn to mush.
You are thirsty
and your spirits lag.
But the path,
both beautiful and endless,
beckons you.
Sprays of feathered ferns

and soft emerald moss,
gurgling brooks,
mushrooms
popping up from the forest floor—
trios of tiny mustard-yellow parasols,
shelves of tawny caps lining rotting limbs,
filmy white pipes—
catch your eye as you trudge,
swatting mosquitoes,
wondering why you came.
Then,
the air grows thin,
ribbons of blue sky draw your gaze.
You push through blackberry bushes,
careless in your haste.
You bleed.
Damn it!
Then you arrive.
A vertical river of white
pours out of the sky.
Heaven slides down
through the trees
like a bride's train.
The water thunders,
whispers.
Don't look for rainbows.
There are none.
The magnificent falls,
dappled with sunlight,
topple through a sea of green.[5]

There are so many positive ways to change a mood. I find the most effective to be to immerse myself in Beauty, which can mean anything from visiting an art gallery to taking a hike. In his poem "Ode on a Grecian Urn," John Keats wrote, "Beauty is truth, / truth Beauty,— / that is all / Ye know on earth / and all ye need to know."[6] A sure-fire way to lighten a dark mood is to be in Nature. It doesn't need to be a glorious spring day. The weather can be rainy or hot, but if you open your eyes to Nature, you are sure to find something of beauty that you can focus on. When I go for walks, I like to take my phone with me so I can take pictures of the botanical friends I meet along the way. I notice how the red berries are now more brilliant than they were just days ago, how the magnolia buds are forming on the trees, how crows wheel across the sky in a huge circle while squirrels hop on the telephone wires as if they are sending Morse code. When I look at waterfalls, rainbows, stars, I do not think about myself—and this is a good thing. I do not brood on my finances or relationships, my job or lack of sleep. Instead, I watch how the moon spills into a space in the sky and hear the owl question the night. In my opinion—and experience—there is nothing a good walk won't make better.

Of course, if you are too tired to walk or it's a blizzard outside, there is beauty to be found in music, all kinds of music. I am partial to Rachmaninoff's "Piano Concerto No. 2 in C Minor, op. 18." I remember hearing it one day when I was putting apples on a display. I was working in a fruit and vegetable store in Cambridge, Massachusetts, at the time. That piece came on and I was totally elevated out of myself, my puny complaints, and my dissatisfactions. The violins surged together, moving through the air like the most magnificent ship. The bass made my groin ache with desire. I almost forgot to breathe.

There is other less cerebral music that lifts me as well. I love big band music. I dance around the house with my earphones and a mop, swinging and singing, laughing away. And the Joan Baez station on Pandora has all my old favorite tunes and takes me down memory lane. Sometimes *too* much. The point is, music can change your mood, and does. Which is why sometimes I refuse to listen, because I want to stay stuck. I choose to wallow in whatever has me down. If that's your story, be my guest, but in my experience, that doesn't work. It just closes the shutters and pulls down the blinds, and darkness falls again.

꙳

My father's solution to any problem was to "Throw the cat out, drink a cup of tea, and read a good book." Leaving the poor cat aside, I think the latter two suggestions are good ones. Making a good strong cup of tea, or whatever beverage you choose for yourself, and sitting down with a good book is a wonderful way to light up. In taking this action, you are telling yourself that you needn't always be running around accomplishing things. You are a human *being,* as they say, not a human *doing.* When you stop taking charge and stop falling prey to negativity, you are humbled in a very good way.

When I say, "humbling," I am not talking about being humiliated. I am talking about recognizing that we are all just ordinary people doing spectacular things. I know when I start to charge into activities, the next thing to come will be disregard for other things. Just now, five minutes ago, I shattered our glass brownie pan by putting it under cold water while it was still fresh from the oven, all because I had editing on my mind. I wanted to get this section done before I moved on to the next thing—making succotash for tonight's dinner—before my husband came home from work. Now: no brownie pan and a lot of explaining to do. I have moved no faster on my book.

After these kinds of careless mistakes, I feel remorse and isolation, which just feeds my depression and negativity more. So, I have taken a suggestion from Bilbo Baggins and other Brits: enjoy a cup of tea and a biscuit, and stop thinking you are more important than you really are. Stop taking yourself so seriously. And if in your reading you find a good novel or poetry manuscript, or some excellent narrative nonfiction, you may even find yourself caught up in a world outside your own for a spell, which is always a good thing. Personally, I find Mary Oliver's poetry to be very uplifting. I won't name too many books because there are so many good ones, but if you haven't read them yet, I recommend *All the Light We Cannot See* and *The Help*. (As I read over those titles, I see just how telling they are.)

༄

Circling back to the bad boyfriend, my dad, and even to my current husband in the first decades of our marriage—the best and most important way I have been able to let light into my life, and thus allow others to experience light in theirs, is to take care of *myself*. Let me repeat that: Take. Care. Of. Myself. I have quested over the years to discover just what it is that floats my boat. I have found that simple things like a daily walk, scrambled eggs with maple syrup for breakfast, swimming laps or water aerobics, reading a good book, and making my bed daily are just some of the things that make me happy. Of course, taking my medication as prescribed is a must. I no longer say yes to exercising the way other people may think I should, or eating things I know I won't enjoy—even when they are gifts. I don't wear clothes that make me feel frumpy, fat, or old. And I have learned to set boundaries for myself in my relationships, which doesn't mean I shut people out. It means I have learned how to say "maybe" or "not now" instead of "yes" all the time. I no longer depend on others to make me happy. I create my own happiness and my own joy.

Let the light shine in!

༄

This is obviously not an exhaustive study of the steps that can be taken to bring light into your life, but I have mentioned a few of the things that have worked for me. As I bring this chapter to a close, I think about one other tool that has been so useful in lighting up my life and moving me forward on my journey toward self-transformation and that is Julia Cameron's bestselling book, *The Artist's Way*. I started working with *The Artist's Way* in 1998, just after my father died and I had relapsed into that near-fatal manic episode. Coming up from the ashes of those two events, I was desperate for something, someone who could give me direction, set my life back on course. *The Artist's Way* did just that. I took Cameron's suggestions very seriously. I wrote, and have written, almost every day since that time, three pages in my journal every morning. I have taken myself on artist's dates in which I got to know more about myself and my likes and dislikes on each trip. I have read through every chapter and answered all the questions on several different occasions, created all the collages, danced, sang, whatever it asked me to do. I have done this again and again. I have even led women's groups, using the text and its sequel, *The Vein of Gold*. If this all sounds like a lot of work, it is and it isn't. If it is work, that's only because it requires commitment and consistency. Creative play changed me, lit me up, and helped me become who I am meant to be. If there is one thing that I feel has facilitated my transformation, it is this book.

TOOLKIT #3

LIGHT is a beautiful thing. It can transform those dark, scary shadows under the stairs into the welcoming corners they really are. Of course, it goes without saying that darkness is sometimes necessary. We learn the most from our darkest times ... that is if we can just keep ourselves moving forward and trust that there will be light ahead. If I have done one thing right in my life, it is to keep on keeping on, despite major setbacks and adversity. Bipolar disorder darkened me, but it didn't get me down. Alcoholism clobbered me, but I fought back and carried on. Rejection, illness, depression? I walked on through, and all because there is light. I have seen it. I feel it. I know it. I choose to walk into it.

Here are some suggested practices to lead you into the light:

BE HONEST. In recovery circles, the saying goes that *the* key to success lies in the individual's ability to be honest with themselves and others. It is this rigorous honesty that pulls back the curtains on a life, revealing the bogus wizard who is desperately trying to manipulate reality. Once this great reveal has taken place, light can shine on our lives and illuminate a path toward an authentic self. "So, what's the big deal?" you might ask. "It is easy to be honest. Just don't lie!" But here's the rub—what is the truth? For myself, in my addiction, I had piled up so many layers of fabrication, I didn't know what was actually true anymore. Add to that my bipolar disorder and its frequently fantastical thinking, and the lines between imagination and reality blurred.

For a long time, I was lost in the lies I told myself, about myself and about everyone around me. I was simultaneously the most talented, beautiful, and seductive woman on the planet and a useless, ugly piece of no-good shit. I lied to myself about the people I associated with, turning them into the players I needed them to be in the game of the day. Looking for a reason to drink, I made myself a victim in a family where I felt unappreciated and unloved. Looking for ego inflation, I ingratiated myself with celebrities.

Emmy-award-winning actress Blanche Baker was one of my "best friends" in college. As was Oscar-winning filmmaker Debra Chasnoff. I hung with award-winning playwright and author Tom Cole, and his filmmaker wife, Joyce Chopra. I sought out classes and lectures with famous authors like Andre Dubus, Richard Yates, and Derek Walcott, thinking their fame would rub off on me. It seemed that many men I had relations with were either former Olympic rowing champions, theatre producers and directors, or poets laureate. I once "dated" an old man (he was seventy-eight; I was nineteen) who was the grandfather of a super star on a popular television sitcom. None of this really had anything to do with me. These were their own achievements, their own realities, but I acted as if somehow their celebrity made me just that bit more special, that bit more worthwhile as a human being.

It was never enough just to be me.

I lied to myself about my own importance; I was never just one of the girls. I deceived myself and others about everything—my weight, my name, my marital status, my exercise routine, my talent. I did all this in an effort to create a *persona* that I could live with, one that seemed larger than life, better than I really was. The tragic truth is I spent decades being someone I was not, when my genuine self wasn't so bad after all.

When I stopped drinking and later went on medication for my bipolar disorder, the lying slowed down, but it didn't stop entirely. I had to watch myself carefully and frequently amend my conversations, saying, "That's not exactly true. Here's what really happened." I ran three miles not ten. I ate four cookies instead of one. I spent fifty dollars not five. And so on. I found as I became more honest with myself about the little lies, my integrity swelled. I was no longer tempted to shoplift or to hit on someone's father or spouse. I began to recognize that life, as it *really* was, was pretty darn good. I didn't have to make it any better, fancier, more interesting. I accepted responsibility for my life as it was.

Pema Chödrön, a Buddhist teacher and nun, speaks to the process of learning to tell the truth in her book *Comfortable with Uncertainty*. In one chapter she writes, "Taking this kind of responsibility is another way of talking about awakening … because part of taking responsibility is being able to see things very clearly. Another part of taking responsibility is gentleness, which goes along with not judging yourself but rather looking gently and honestly at yourself …."[7] Although Chödrön is not specifically addressing honesty, her words speak to the topic on several levels.

TAKE RESPONSIBILITY. This is the first step in cultivating honesty. I had to take responsibility for my own life, and no longer shirk or evade my truth. Responsibility necessitates letting go of blame, even though we may have been harmed. To blame others is to make oneself a victim, and it is hard to see the truth if we have positioned ourselves as such.

Another obstacle to taking personal responsibility is fear. I spent years dipping and diving to get away from the truth because I was so afraid of what I might find. What if, at the end of all my seeking, I had turned out to be the monster I was afraid I was? In many ways, my self-examination has revealed that truth to me. But, I am here to say, you don't need to be afraid if you are willing to try to live a life based on spiritual principles.

The Universe is forgiving.

EMBRACE GENTLENESS. If fear runs rampant, gentleness calms it. And light. When I shine the spotlight on myself, I may see some stuff I don't like a whole lot, but it is important—vital—to be gentle with myself. To recognize that I am human. I have my assets and my weaknesses. I can embrace them both. This does not mean letting myself or anyone else off the hook, nor does it mean condoning bad behavior. What it means is accepting that all of us are flawed, we all make mistakes. So, we must treat ourselves and others with compassion, at the same time requiring ourselves and others to take responsibility for our errors and rectifying them when we can.

When I embrace my own humanity, I develop compassion for those around me. The world is a better place. Looking more gently at myself allows me to move forward. As I have said before, I believe all creatures respond more favorably to a hug than to a stick. Now I know that when I do something stupid, thoughtless, or dishonest, I no longer have to beat myself up. I give myself a hug and ask, "What's really going on?" I allow myself to make mistakes, something I never did before, and then to take responsibility for them. I allow others to make mistakes too.

SEEK CLARITY. Seeing clearly and with compassion is like opening black curtains that have been drawn all winter and kept the sunlight out. Suddenly, life is no longer grim but rather full of new possibilities and discoveries. How can we practice seeing clearly? I believe we have to have outside help. My own vision is often clouded by the filters I have developed since youth. In order to fully comprehend a situation, I often need a second opinion from someone with more perspective than myself. And there are occasions on which I can catch myself and provide that clearer vision. When I practice compassion and recognize that all sentient beings suffer, as I suffer, from a limited vision of themselves and others, then I can put down my boxing gloves, rest my hands at heart center, and bow my head. More often than not, though, I rely on wise friends to set me on the right path.

EAT YOUR DAILY BREAD: In the Lord's Prayer, we pray, "Give us this day our daily bread." We aren't praying for yesterday; we aren't praying for tomorrow. We are praying that *this* day, and only this day, we will be given exactly what we need to grow and thrive. Every morning when I rise, I ask that God's will, not mine, be done. I believe God's will is for me to be honest with myself and others. So, all day long, I monitor my words and actions, constantly taking inventory of how I am doing, amending errors along the way, or suffering from not doing so. Does this sound like a lot of work? A preoccupation with self? It is, in the best sense. No work of art was ever created without a whole lot of effort. What is the saying? "Art is one percent inspiration, ninty-nine percent perspiration." We are masterpieces in the making. Becoming those masterpieces requires a lot of work, but it is work that can be enjoyable and is always very rewarding.

I love it when I catch myself about to do or say something that is contrary to my best growth. I feel like a young plant sending new, healthy shoots into the Universe. The good news is this practice is manageable when I focus on one day at a time. If I take on more than the twenty-four hours ahead, during eight of which I will be sleeping, I become overwhelmed and discouraged. But living in a "day-tight compartment," as the great motivator Dale Carnegie said, enables me to use this spiritual tool and to move forward on my path.[8]

CHAPTER 4
Updating The Hardwired Mind

When you are remodeling a house, one of the most important things you need to look into is the wiring. You may already be aware that the wiring needs updating if fuses are blowing or there is a burning smell you can't account for. You may even have been shocked on occasion when you plugged in a cord or turned on a lamp. These are all signs you need to call an electrician to get the job done.

With people, it is not always as easy to detect faulty wiring. What we accept as someone's personality might actually be a defect in their thinking that they need to address. Those irrational outbursts may be more than just a teenager's hormones. A vicious verbal attack might not just signify the result of a poor night's sleep. These actions may actually be signals that we, or someone we love, is suffering from some "quirk" of the brain. It may be time to call in the experts.

⁊

So when did all this wiring go bad? For myself, I believe bad messages had been passed down for generations, along with alcoholism and mental illness. Rigid thinking and false ideas were the legacy that affected some in my family more than others. In my family of origin, we were all the victims of my mother's catastrophic thinking, the surety that the other shoe was about to drop at any moment. She, I am certain, inherited this way of thinking from someone in her own family of origin. Plus, there is the story that my mother, at one time in her youth, was turned away by a card reader who found her future too tragic to share. Whatever the cause, the tendency to think this way followed us throughout our lives.

My husband likes to tell the story of the roast beef. One day, his mother was making roast beef for dinner. His father was partial to the well-done ends of the roast, and he asked if he might have them. To which his mother responded, "There are no ends." "Why not?" his father asked. "Because I cut them off," she replied. "Why?" he asked. "Because that's the way my mother cooked it," she stated and went on cooking. Later, she asked *her* mother why she had cut the ends off the roast beef. "Because that's the way my mother did it," her mother replied. My father's mother kept asking through the generations until she came to her great grandmother. "Great grandmother," she asked, "why do we cut the ends off the roast beef?" "Oh, that's simple," she replied. "I never had a pot big enough for a whole one."

Like a sponge, I soaked up the faulty wiring, holding the superficial lies to my heart, cultivating a life where either sparks flew or the lights simply went out. I told myself I was unloved, too fat, not smart enough, overly selfish, a winner, a loser, nothing. The biggest lie I bought into was the one that told me wealth, fame, and fortune could bring me happiness. I spent decades in painful pursuit of each one.

Ever since I was a child, one piece of faulty wiring in my brain had always told me I wasn't loved. I knew who *was* loved though—my neighbor's daughter. I was about seven years old when I watched her, then nearly two, in her crib. She was a beautiful little girl with chestnut curls and bright blue eyes. I babysat for her sometimes, as a helper, while her mother prepared dinner or washed the clothes. I wonder if that mother ever knew how jealous I was of her only child.

That was just it. The only-child thing. That little girl had no siblings, while I had five sisters, plus all the boys and girls at the school where my father was chaplain who looked to Mom and Dad as surrogate parents. Add to that the fact that my sisters taunted me, told me I was adopted, swore I didn't belong because I was different. I was the only blonde in a family of brunettes. I was flighty, bratty, bitchy, and possessive. Of course, that wasn't the real reason they rejected me. No one knew the real reason yet, nor would anyone know until I was forty-three years old: I had bipolar disorder. I might as well have been from Mars.

Still, the message that I was not wanted became embedded in me, and I acted out. I became a liar and a thief. I destroyed my sisters' property. I dreamed of running away. I rationalized: if I couldn't have my neighbor's life, I would at least have her things. Never the stuffed koala bear I had lusted after, swearing someday I would have one of my own. No, I stole her colorful books—the Dr. Seuss and P.D. Eastman *I CAN READ* titles that came in the mail once a month. I would go to the faculty mailroom to retrieve them, and instead of bringing them back to the little girl, I would rip open the cardboard casing, look through *Ten Apples Up on Top* and *Hop on Pop*, then throw the books away. I would tell her mother that nothing had come. Eventually, she cancelled her daughter's subscription.

In retrospect, I see those actions as another signal at play. In our family of six girls, my mother assigned us each a role. My oldest sister was the matriarch, the one assigned to keep us together. Sister number two was the poet and writer. Number three was the musician, singer, and artist. I, number four, was the actress. (The irony is not lost there.) By the time sisters number five and six came along, Mom had either given up or relaxed her role-assigning duties. They were allowed to do pretty much whatever they chose to do.

These assignments were restricting, not only to me but to my sisters, I believe. They clipped my wings when all I wanted to do was fly, to express myself in so many ways. I think, in retrospect, my mother's attitude about these roles might have contributed to my later limited notion of God. In my father's world, God was all magic, incense, music, stained glass, and mystery. Every time I went to church with my father I asked, "How?" My connection with God was wide open and filled with wonder. But with my mother's seemingly more limited, dark vision, all I asked was, "Why?" Why was I discouraged from writing? Why was I not allowed to follow my dreams? Why did I have to limit myself? Perhaps these are questions my mother asked herself throughout her life, a life cut short by a freak accident when she was sixty-nine. Perhaps she knew all along that, for her, there would be no happy ending, and she was trying to protect us from the same. I will never know.

When I threw out my neighbor's books, it was as if I was saying, "There is only room for one reader in this relationship ... and it is me." I wanted to deprive her of something that brought her pleasure, just as I had been deprived of my love for writing and singing for so long, living in the shadow of what felt like a childhood prison.

৵

Speaking of prison, my faulty wiring almost landed me in big trouble. The summer I was eight, my mother, sisters, and I went to Block Island to vacation with friends. I found the beach boring. Neither Mom nor her friend, Betty, really planned our beach outings, so we had no food and not enough to drink. I was hungry and thirsty. So, I left the beach, without telling anyone, and went to work at the souvenir shop in hopes of making enough money for a soda. The lady who owned the shop was always looking for kids to come in and help out during the day. I worked for what seemed like hours. When I told the store owner I was going to leave, she thanked me for my efforts—I had stocked shelves, straightened magazines, swept floors, and so forth—but she gave me *nothing,* not even a nickel. I was so mad, I took the nearest thing I could and stuffed it in my pocket. It was a bottle of hot pink nail polish. I ran all the way back to our cottage, sat on my bed with the rib cord bedspread imprinting itself on my legs like bars, and put the polish on my nails.

The next thing I knew, the police were outside the house. I thought for sure they had come to arrest me. Hands balled into fists, my face burning red, I stared at the floor as they explained that Mom had sent them to find me. She thought I had drowned. They took me back to the beach, still thirsty, still hungry.

Coincidentally, the first poem I ever wrote, typed out on a piece of manila paper and cut into a neat square, was written later that year:

OCTOBER 26, 1963

Had no lunch,
Hurt head,
Cried and cried.
Hopie Costin,
Ps– Is very hungry.

The message: *I'll never get what I want*, has haunted me all my life, even as a child. So has its companion: *I am owed*. The behavior that drives me to take all that I can, on my own, and to trust no one, is another faulty signal I have tried to rewire.

و

As time went on, I found my mind was giving me plenty of bad information on its own. The thing about bipolar disorder is there are two sides—the *up* and the *down*—and there is little middle ground in between, until you are properly medicated and attended to. When I was *down,* the ordinary messages—*I am a failure; I will always screw up; I will never get over this*—that come to anyone who is feeling a little blue came to me. However, they had an intensity like a runaway locomotive; they derailed my thinking. A little comment like, "It looks like you've put on a few pounds," became years of anorexia and bulimia. I am not talking about the months during my junior year in high school when I ate nothing, drank only tea, and shrunk down to about one hundred pounds (not a good weight for my sturdy English frame). Instead, what I *heard*—"We would love you if you were thinner"—precipitated years when I kept a lemon-soap mix in the fridge to induce vomiting and joined programs and diets that had me eating thimbles of greens and teaspoons of protein. My family, all but one sister, watched and said nothing. Later in my twenties, I ran fifteen miles a day and even snuck in to run the Boston Marathon (which I finished in 3:27:0-something). For some, this might seem like the ideal weight-loss plan. For me, it was disastrous. All I ever thought about was how fat I felt, no matter how small I *actually* was. My faulty wiring drove me to obsess over the numbers on the scale, the size of my thighs. That was no way to live.

Neither was the swing in the opposite direction when I binged and blew up to an XXL, hovering around 180 pounds when I was in college. Weight was not the issue though. My insecurity and self-loathing were based on the messages that came from growing up with a mother who struggled with her own self-image and installed the buttons of self-loathing and perfectionism in me. Put on a diet in the third grade, I knew then that if I was fat, I was unlovable. I may have only imagined it, but my mother always seemed to serve me far smaller portions than those of my sisters. By the time I was stuffed into a pea-green school uniform and looking like a round pod, I had developed a hatred for myself that consumed me. In my late teens and twenties, I sought solace from the belief that I could never be loved by having sex with countless men, one of whom said to me, when I asked him what he was thinking after we had finished, "I wish you had lost weight." He could have been my mother speaking. She would always ask when I called home from college, "How much do you weigh?"

I am pleased to say this negative message has been eradicated. In the chapter, "Faulty Plumbing," I will address the issue of feeding ourselves a healthy, balanced diet. Suffice it to say that for dinner recently my family ate salmon, kale and spinach, and carrots.

Not an unusual meal for us. When my son walked in with a Key lime pie and asked me if I wanted a piece, I didn't hesitate. Of course! I ate it and I loved it. But more of that later.

৵

Another message that haunted me when I was in the throes of depression was, *You don't have the right to live.* This one makes me so sad. I think of all the souls out there who are suffering in a space so dark, they don't know which way to turn. When my husband and I lived in Michigan in the early 2000s, two of my friends in the neighborhood died by suicide—one overdosed; the other threw herself in front of a moving train. At the same time, the sister of my son's friend hanged herself. Insensitive observers blame the act of suicide on the weakness of the victim. I am here to tell you, people with mental disorders are not weak at all. Rather, they are powerless over the illness that has set out to kill them.

I can vividly remember times in my teens and twenties when I ran from myself, terrified that the evil voices, the demons in my head, would push me in front of a car or out a window. I imagined that somehow, I would get a knife and really slit my wrists this time. Calling myself back from the edge was a visceral exercise. Honestly, I don't know how I survived some of those times. I guess I was appropriately named.

Somehow, I have clung to Hope.

۰٫

I'd like to share a dream with you that I had when I was fifteen. It was one of those prophetic dreams that lingers long after it is over. Its message has sustained me over the years. I see everything as clearly now as on the day I woke sitting up in bed, sweating profusely, the sheets tossed all over my bedroom.

۰٫

I was walking up a set of narrow concrete stairs in a stone turret when I got to a door. I knocked and a voice said, "Enter!" so I went in.

Inside was a hexagonal-shaped room. There was no furniture, just a marble slab of a table in the middle. Nothing else. A henchman with a hood and axe stood by the table and motioned for me to lie down. I did. He moved my long, blonde hair to the table's edge.

"Are you ready?" he asked.

"I am," I replied.

As if I were floating outside my body, I watched as he brought the axe down through my neck. The sharpened steel felt cold. I could smell the blood as it gushed from my neck, but I felt no pain.

Suddenly, I knew I had made a great mistake.

"This is wrong!" I cried. "I don't want to die!"

He told me if I could keep my head on as I traveled through a black tunnel, I would live. I thanked him, got down from the table, holding my head on tight, and entered the tunnel.

The tunnel was full of cobwebs and dirt, and I could barely breathe. People howled and cried—shrieks and moans, babbling, asylum sounds. For the longest time, I crawled as hands came out of nowhere and tugged at me, trying to pull me down, but I persisted. Finally, just as I was about to give up, I saw a pinprick of light.

The pinprick never got any bigger the closer I got. But when I reached it, I saw it was a paper hoop. I stepped through it—like a lioness in the circus—out into a beautiful, technicolor scene. Mountains and emerald grass, crisp air and sunshine. A red barn. My two younger sisters (or were they my daughters as yet unborn?) were playing in the lower field, blowing dandelions. I waved to them with both hands over my head. They waved back and came running.

My head did not fall off.

꒰

I haven't thought about that dream for a long time, but I can now see how it was a metaphor for my life. My depression wanted me dead. All those hands and voices, the bad messages of my disorder, wanted to drag me down. I have had to fight my way through the faulty wiring all my life. When someone else might hear, "It is going to be hard," my disorder tells me, "It's going to be impossible. You will never make it. You are just not good enough. Loser." Such harsh voices are always beating me *down*.

... That is, unless they are beating me *up*. Rumor has it that mania can be a "pleasant" thing. Certainly, in its early stages when the flush of enthusiasm is just building, mania can be exciting and energizing. But I liken it to booze and alcoholism: the first drink may seem like a good idea, there may be a little glow, but soon enough, the police are called in, noses are broken, and marriages are destroyed. It never ends well.

Mania initially promises me that I will be creative, successful, happy. But those are the kinds of lies that come with a hefty price tag. In truth, mania brings pain. It doesn't have to be full-blown mania either—the kind where you believe yourself to be Chris Evert at Wimbledon or you "fall in love" with someone totally inappropriate because your sick mind has told you they are a god. (Actually, the man is a sleazy, immoral, self-serving cheat who preys on sick women. But that's another story.) *That* kind of mania spends thousands of dollars in minutes and tears families apart. I know. I have been there, done that, got the handcuffs. Thank God for a husband and children who have stuck with me despite it all so we could get to the other side. And I really do want to show you how we got to the other side.

First, let me say this about mania: even less-pronounced mania terrifies me because of the lies it tells me about myself. These lies are so painful because they are so extreme. For example, my mania tells me that I will win an Oscar. It has me believing that it will be so, that I need to get the dress, write the speech, hire the stylist—immediately. Now everyone thinks about what they'd like to wear and what they'd say if they won, don't they? That's the fun of Oscar parties. You drink a little champagne and giggle as you think about how you could be Meryl Streep up there. After all, she's just human. (I think.) We all imagine, we all dream. That's what humans do. But we don't all dream the way mania dreams. Mania dreams with a big stick that beats you up and has you in tears when you don't succeed at something impossible.

Never mind that I have actually written six feature films. Forget that Paramount was interested in one and that I collaborated with a Hollywood producer on another. Mania tells me that until I have that statue in my hand, until my books are *New York Times* bestsellers, until I make appearances on *Oprah*, *The Ellen DeGeneres Show*, and *60 Minutes*, until my face is on the cover of *People* magazine, I am nothing. Making impossible demands, mania pretends to be creative but is actually very cruel. It sets me up for depression, and the cycle begins again. Now don't get me wrong. I think having goals is very important. There is a difference, however, between having reasonable, thought-out goals and flying off into la-la land on the Mania Express.

~

When I was in my early twenties, I was riding high in my early writing career ... or so I thought. What I was really doing was drinking profusely and associating with famous writers. And those writers had great hopes for me. I did too. But the combination of booze and bipolar disorder ripped any chance to succeed away as I froze in the beams of two anonymous snipers: alcoholism and mania. They told me I was better than I was while depression fed my insecurity and stifled me. Then, when I got sober, I stopped writing all together. I equated being creative with getting drunk.

So, how have I moved from all this bad wiring into being a happy, serene, loving wife and mother, and a prolific, confident, successful writer?

The first step in moving from crazy to complete was to recognize that I have a crazy mind. In the past, I have gotten my feathers ruffled when my husband has told me that I am, in fact, mentally ill. *Not me!* I want to shout. *I am a very capable, successful, amazing woman.* All true. But how much more capable, successful and amazing can I be if I first accept my limitations? There is absolutely nothing to suggest that someone with treated bipolar disorder and alcoholism cannot go on to live a productive, creative, awesome life. Not a *normal* life. There will always be the illnesses to contend with. But a totally satisfying life? Yes!

I didn't live that way for many years. I wore my mental illness like a shroud, both terrified and resentful of its characteristics. Every once in a while, I would stick my toes in the water, taking on a part-time teaching job. Volunteering. With every experience, I proved to myself that I could handle a little bit more without going over the edge. But I veered away from too much creativity. That seemed too explosive for me. Until recently, during the last five years.

ॐ

When I was let go from my full-time teaching position, I was both embarrassed and elated. The job was killing me from the inside out. Every day, when I stood in front of my four classes of thirty-five high school students, I felt like a fraud. This wasn't me. This was somebody else's dream for me, to have stability, a steady income, a regular job. But I couldn't bring "regular" into the job, and it got me in trouble. I was too creative. Too much outside the box. I didn't fit. I heard that message every day for five years. I was glad to be done with soldiering through, because that's when my husband's health took a turn for the worst.

In hindsight, it was a good thing I lost my job. I could now be there to care for Thom when he most needed me. In 2015, he came out on the other side of liver cancer, with a preowned lady liver. He too had been in a job where the messages were primarily negative and the situation had dragged him down. But on June 30, 2015, he was given a new chance at living. The most significant thing was that he had his mind back, the mind fog was gone, which enabled him to adopt a new perspective on life. From that moment on, he has chosen, every day, to live his life to the fullest.

With Thom as my guide, I latched on to his new found health, faith, and optimism. I believed it was my chance to be reborn too. Tired of believing the old lies about how I should be living my life, avoiding any triggers that might offset another devastating manic episode, I picked up my pen and began, tentatively, to write. I accompanied Thom to a conference in September

2015, sat by the pool while he attended workshops and luncheons and, in five days, penned the first draft of a novel later to be published as *When the Moon Winks*.

It was a start.

There are some things worth taking a risk for, and I am—you are—one of them. By opening myself up to my creative side, I was in jeopardy of summoning old demons that could potentially have had a disastrous effect. But that didn't happen. I haven't had a full-blown manic episode, or depression, since then. Nor have I had the desire to pick up a drink.

⌁

I have talked a lot about bipolar disorder and alcoholism in this chapter. But what of those who don't suffer from these (or other) illnesses, and still struggle with faulty wiring in their brains? What about the person who is driven by the need to be at the top of their career? Who feels unsatisfied unless they are number one? And what of the people who accumulate great masses of wealth and material goods in the chase for Happiness, only to find they feel empty inside? Nothing is enough. Then there are those who insist on being right and judge harshly when others deviate from their visions. There are so many others who suffer from the faulty messages that filter through their brains. So, what can any of us, *all* of us, do to rewire our thinking and tune in to happier, pleasurable, more joyful lives?

The first step in any positive change is Honesty. When we look at a house, we take an honest inventory of what does and does not need to be changed. In a human, this is not as easy as you might think. We have so many layers of denial built up, so many lies that we have believed and lived by—or even told. So, maybe we need to go back to step zero, which is *"to ask."*

Step zero doesn't necessarily mean you ask for anything specific. It just means you ask someone—or something, anything—for help. "What do I need to know about myself?" "What bad messages clutter my brain?" "What do I need to do?" I would be a liar if I told you that my entire recovery was my own doing. I have needed help from Day One. And I have asked for help—from the God of my understanding, from friends, family, books, fortune cookies, and even license plates. I will take direction from wherever I can find it, and it can be found everywhere. I've found that you just have to ask and it will come. I pray for a lot of things— and a lot of people—but mostly I pray that I will be open to guidance, care, and love. That opens the door to many things. Writing this book, for instance, whose time had come. When I put my bipolar disorder and my alcoholism out there in the Universe, I know I will be given everything I need to handle them today. Without that simple action, I continue to try to run the show. And we all know where that leads.

༄

One of the other most effective tools in rewiring the brain, whether you have a mental disorder or not, is Discipline. Ralph Waldo Emerson wrote, "A foolish consistency is the hobgoblin of little minds." Sorry, Ralph, I beg to differ. I know that feeling firsthand, of shying away from routine because it stifles creativity. However, I have found it to be truer that routine enables my creativity to flourish and my illnesses to stay in check. It's all about *balance*. Most everyone who knows me knows that on any given day, I am up between four and four thirty in the morning. I drink my coffee, say my prayers, write in my journal, and work. We eat breakfast around half past six. By 7:15 a.m., we are either at a twelve-step meeting or the gym, depending on the day. Workouts are always done by half past ten, home by eleven. Eat lunch and work. Nap. Of course, there are days when I veer from this, but generally this is my life.

Except today. Today I slept until 6:42 a.m. I chose not to go to the gym this morning. And I am eager to see what the rest of this unusual day brings. The point is, I am not *stuck* in a routine. I use my routine as a guideline. But I can be flexible and go with the flow, without panicking that I have lost time or I will never exercise again. Which was my old way of thinking. Today, I see the supple branches of the trees swaying in the wind. That's what I aim for: sway.

Quite apart from the fact that routine creates balance, it also establishes positive habits, so I don't have to listen to my brain argue about whether or not I should go to the gym. I just do it. Routine takes the bickering out of my brain. It erases those old tapes that tell me I can't.

When I sit down to write, I assume I am going to write at least five pages at a sitting, if not more, because that is what novelist Lawrence Block suggests I do.[9] (Who am I to argue with success?) So far, I have written five books that way. Routine makes life so much easier, so much more fluid as we float from one promise to another, feeling better about ourselves with each step we take. The old bad voices die off and only the positive affirmations remain. Life changes and blooms, like flowers in spring.

ॐ

Speaking of affirmations, nothing works better to wash a dirty brain than a good affirmation. For many years, as I ran during my early recovery, and even now when I swim laps, I say to myself over and over, "Assist Don't Resist" or "Patience and Persistence." These two affirmations have become like the heartbeat that moves blood through my veins. For those of you who may have never used affirmations before, they are just little words or phrases that you say over and over to yourself, possibly to erase negative thoughts or feelings. Julia Cameron's, *The Artist's Way* contains numerous helpful affirmations. For some years, my massage therapist gave me the gift of Louise Hay's *365 Daily Affirmations* calendar for Christmas. I have them plastered all over our house. My favorite tells me that the most important thing I can do today is love myself. This year I have gone with the Dalai Lama calendar, which is not as catchy as Louise but equally thought-provoking.

Whatever it takes to get out of my own head.

I also use positive readings in general: "Happiness Prayer" from Joseph Murphy, the Serenity Prayer, the Prayer of St. Francis. Pema Chödrön. Thich Nhat Hanh. Mary Oliver's poetry. Even Winnie the Pooh. Like I said, *any* positive message to replace the old junk in my brain.

Today, life is astonishing. Sure, some old messages rear their ugly heads. I just pat them and assure them that I won't be needing them anymore. I have a new brain that lets me think about life in a fresh, positive way.

TOOLKIT #4

OPENNESS is the tool that has been most helpful to me in fixing my faulty wiring. For years, even into my sobriety, I clutched onto the "truth" that I needed to be right about everything. If I am really honest with myself, as I urge us all to be, I believed I *was* right about everything. Even if I had no expertise in a subject, I assumed I knew better than everyone else. I walked around with a smug, self-satisfied smirk of superiority, secretly judging others. I might as well have been a paid assassin for the amount of character assassination I engaged in. (Okay, I am exaggerating a bit, but not much.)

The problem with being right about everything was that *I wasn't*. I lost out on a lot of useful instruction and experience by insisting I had all the answers. The truth is, I was afraid not to have all the answers. That fear stems from the perfectionism thing and buying into the notion that in order to justify my place on the planet, I had to be perfect at everything I did. What resulted was that I stopped trying new things because the pressure to succeed was too acute, too painful. So, how was I able to replace the old, faulty wiring with new wiring through openness?

WASH YOUR BRAIN. I realize how extreme that sounds, but think about it. Couldn't your brain use a little washing? I know mine needed it, and still does. Fed for so many years on the poison of negativity, self-deprecation, materialism, self-righteousness, and fear, my mind didn't have a lot to offer me. Sure, I was smart, attended Ivy League schools, and sounded articulate, but none of those factors could eradicate the bad messages that populated my brain. It took coming into a recovery program and being humbled by simple slogans like "Easy Does It" and "First Things First" to reprogram my thinking. Some people argue that twelve-step programs turn the participants into automatons, spouting off simplistic phrases meant for children in elementary school. In my experience, those slogans *saved my ass*. They took the place of bigotry, judgement, and anger and instead created new synapses of hope.

BE CURIOUS. "'Curiouser and curiouser,' cried Alice (she was so much surprised, that for the moment she quite forgot how to speak good English)."[10] This quote, taken from Lewis Carroll's classic *Alice in Wonderland* touches on a characteristic of being open that I find critical to both my success and happiness. Being curious is like having an open parachute and letting the wind take you, effortlessly, to places you've never been. For so many years, my parachute was closed, and I stayed firmly planted in outdated ideas and misconceptions about who I was and what I could do, who other people were and what they were about. But once I took the leap, jumped on the back of openness, and pulled the cord, I found myself able to see and do things in a whole new way. I'm not talking about big things, necessarily, though some have been. I am talking about small things, like being open to trying new recipes instead of grilling all the time, and wearing red and pink instead of the ubiquitous blue I have worn all my life (it brings out the color of my eyes). I have been open to ziplining, white-water rafting, tubing, hiking up big mountains, writing and publishing books, driving on I-77, finding alternatives to driving on I-77, trusting a food program to help me lose weight, experimenting with exercise until I found some that worked for me, learning how to use new technology ... shall I go on? Curiosity has opened so many new doors for me. I wonder sometimes why I sat in the corner for so long, waiting for life to ask me to dance, when all it took was for me to pose the question myself.

EMBRACE SPONTANEITY. This is a sensitive tool for me because I am bipolar. I have to keep a tight watch on spontaneity versus impulsivity and mania. Still, I find spontaneity essential to exercising an open mind. Spontaneity is all about responding to life rather than reacting to it. I respond to the input I am receiving from the Universe. In Richard Le Gallienne's poem "I Meant to Do My Work Today," he writes, "I meant to do my work today— / But a brown bird sang in the apple tree ... And all the leaves were calling me."[11] This seems to be a perfect example of spontaneity. When I am working inside on a hot summer day, cleaning or writing, and I look outside at the diamonds dancing on the pool, I sometimes rip off my clothes and pull on a suit and dive in. I am always glad I did. You know why? Because it makes me laugh and smile and recognize just how fun life can be.

Spontaneity is all about playfulness. It is about letting go of the expectations we may have had for that moment and going in another direction. I find it so liberating to change plans every now and again. When I have prepped everything for dinner and my husband comes home and says he would like to take me out, do I insist we stay home and eat what I have prepared? Hell no! I shove the veggies in the fridge, grab my sweater, and away we go! It's so much more fun not to have to be the boss of everything. Spontaneity has allowed me to welcome the myriad of gifts that come into my life on a regular basis. I have loosened up, lightened up, and let go.

BE RECEPTIVE. Both curiosity and spontaneity have motivated me to experience places and things that I wouldn't ordinarily. They have expanded my outlook and helped me to see that there are so many ways in which I can challenge myself, enjoy my life, that I have left unexplored. But what about opening my intellect? This is where I believe receptivity comes in, for this is the tool that has pried open the closed trunk in my brain where I keep useless information and antiquated ideas. As I have practiced being open, I have attracted new ideas. Very often these ideas are in the form of books. I don't ask for these books. They appear like stray animals, just wandering into my life. Many of them have changed my life indelibly. Take, for example, *The Book of Joy: Lasting Happiness in a Changing World* by the Dalai Lama and Archbishop Desmond Tutu, with Douglas Abrams.

My husband and I were in a bookstore in Vermont several years ago. We were wandering around, browsing as we always do. We were actually looking for audiobooks by Pema Chödrön when I stumbled across *The Book of Joy*. I had never heard of the book, but it made its presence known to me by actually almost falling on my head! I was drawn, inexplicably, to the title and the photo on the cover, so I bought it. Since then, I have read it countless times; it is that good. And I have gifted it to at least a dozen people. The point is, I was receptive when it called to me, and it changed my life. So many other books have influenced me, opened my mind to a new way of seeing, some fiction, some non-fiction. Here is a brief sample: Dante Alighieri's *The Divine Comedy;* M. Scott Peck's *The Road Less Traveled;* Don Miguel Ruiz's *The Four Agreements;* Hermann Hesse's *Siddhartha;* Alexandre Dumas's *The Count of Monte Cristo,* Brené Brown's *The Gifts of Imperfection;* Dale Carnegie's *How to Stop Worrying and Start Living;* Emmett Fox's *The Sermon on the Mount* .... I could go on.

I am not only receptive to books, I am receptive to messages from songs playing on the radio, someone's share at a twelve-step meeting, a postcard from a friend. Chance conversations with strangers can be enlightening. As can deep conversations with friends. The point is, I need to be mindful of whatever comes across my path and look at it as a gift from the Universe, a little clue I am on the right path, or that I've veered off. I see that gift as a message that I am loved.

Our kids had a book as children called *A House Is a House for Me.* The book rocked and rolled throughout its pages, sweeping us along in its cadence until it came to the final page that read, "Each creature that's known has a house of its own / And the earth is a house for us all."[12] I like to think that the Earth—the Universe—has messages for us all, every minute, every day. Our job is to be open and receptive to those messages that help us, always, to become closer to the people we are meant to be.

CHAPTER 5
Fixing Faulty Plumbing

According to rehab experts, if you purchase a home built before the 1960s, you should expect problems with the plumbing. Unless the previous owner has already taken care of replacing old pipes with new galvanized steel ones, those old pipes will bear the scars of misuse, not because the previous tenants were malicious. Rather, they were uninformed. Who knew back then that putting paint, cleaning products, and toxic chemicals down a drain could be harmful not only to the plumbing but also to the environment? Today, we are educated about not dumping old medications down drains and into the water table or pouring fat and grease directly into the system. These actions not only clog the pipes, they harm wildlife as well. On every women's room stall is a sign cautioning women not to put feminine products and diapers down the toilet as that will cause the system to back up and overflow. The same can be said of paper towels, cotton balls, and scrub pads. Plumbing is a delicate thing and needs to be treated with respect. This is true of our human plumbing too.

ᘒ

I am a pre-1960s model human. Born in 1955, I grew up in the era of Twinkies, when every adult man or woman carried a cigarette in one hand and a cocktail in the other. Fatty foods, smokes, and booze were the norm back then. The great movie stars of the day were always filmed with their eyes squinting from the smoke that rose in tendrils around their backlit faces. Cinema made cigarettes seem so seductive. Even today, and though I am not a smoker, when my husband and I have been intimate, I will quip, "I need a cigarette." I am joking … but I am not. That propaganda stuck with me and many others.

Of course, we have all heard the statistics: more than 480,000 people die each year from illnesses caused by cigarette smoking; secondhand smoke causes more than 41,000 deaths each year. This equates to more than 1,300 deaths every day.[13] My personal experience with lung disease stems from my eleventh-grade math class.

As a junior in high school, on track for a good college, I was required to take Algebra 2 / Trigonometry. Now math and I never got along. I was a little more inclined to understand geometry, somehow it appealed to the poet in me, but algebra you could keep. I barely passed algebra 1 in my freshman year, and the idea of taking algebra 2 / Trig gave me the sweats.

When I walked into class the first day, I knew I was doomed. Our teacher, an older man bent at the waist with a hound-dog face and runny eyes, shall remain anonymous. Suffice it to say, he had emphysema, attributed to his smoking, and spent a large part of the class coughing up who knows what into his white hanky and then running out of the room to quickly light up a smoke. He had zero tolerance for questions, of which I had many, and whenever I would ask him one, he would get red in the face and cough so violently, we all expected him to keel right over. Not wanting to be the cause of his demise, I stopped asking questions, scraped by with my father's help, and swore I would never take math again.

I blame my gaps in further mathematical education on the cigarettes.

My mother smoked. A lot. I think it was her way of trying to stay thin, for that was always the message that came with smoking back then. It may be true; I don't know. I do know she smoked enough to turn four of my five sisters and me off it altogether. The sixth sister gave up smoking some years ago. I wouldn't be surprised if, one day, one of us turned up with spots on our lungs from secondhand smoke. Stranger things have happened.

So where am I going with all this? And what do cigarettes have to do with faulty plumbing?

If you imagine that our organs are like the pipes in the house, and our mouths are the drain into which we are putting sometimes destructive things, then you will see why anything that goes in our mouths—cigarettes, booze, food, and more—has the potential to mess with our "plumbing." Being human, we also have the added factor of our brains, because nothing happens in our bodies without the mind-body connection. For example, when my mother lit up a cigarette, immediately you could see conflict arise in her. She wanted to smoke, but she hated it at the same time. She liked how it suppressed her appetite, but she was ashamed by what she saw as a weakness, and she was always opening windows and flapping her arms at the smoke, or apologizing, or worse yet, standing out on the porch in freezing weather, puffing away. Her mind wouldn't let her simply enjoy what she was doing. If we were harsh judges of her habit, she was harsher still.

꒰

The "critical parent" in my mother's mind infiltrated her interactions with us as children. We were her six perfect girls—each assigned a role in the family. She fed us the party line we were to carry with us all our lives; we took her words in through our mouths and swallowed them, believing what we were told, only to find that those beliefs actually had nothing to do with reality. ... Okay, I should speak for myself. My mother's beliefs had nothing to do with *my* reality. She led me to believe I was fat, and most of my memories of my mother center around how she treated me and my size. In third grade, she put me on my first diet, sending me to school with a "healthy lunch." I tricked her. Every day I would trade my apple and sandwich for money from kids at school to buy ice cream from the vending machine in the cafeteria. At dinner, she served me portions of food that were half the size of my sisters'.

I don't think I would have minded the food rationing if only her love hadn't been portioned out too. I always had the feeling that she couldn't love me unless I was thin—probably more my reality than hers. But, honestly, the only time I remember my mother taking me shopping was when I was anorexic and down to 104 pounds. I remember her telling me how pretty I looked. I had literally starved for her love. Mom had a funny way of being interested.

What felt like her judgement was always hurtful. When I think about it, I hurt for years because food, for the longest time, was my primary addiction. Whether eating it or not eating it, it didn't matter; food was always on my mind. Even today, when I think about places I have been and people I have been with, I think about food. It's *always* there.

The same year my mother put me on my first diet, we bought a farm in Vermont and went there for the summer. One of the places we frequented was the Vermont Country Store in Weston. For a kid, the store was magic. Open bins of penny candy that you could scoop out into little paper bags beckoned to you. Only it wasn't so magic for me. All the wax straws and bubble gum, the Swedish Fish and chocolate drops called me, but I knew my mother was watching. I knew I needed to be good. So, I bought a pickle for five cents and ate it all the way home, long after everyone else had finished their sweets, taunting my sisters. I knew then the perverse pride of deprivation, something that would stick with me for many years.

In high school, I tried the grapefruit and egg diet; the Carnation Slender Diet; the Stillman Diet. I ate only cheese soufflé. And, as mentioned before, I purged, using that mixture made of lemon juice, soap, and water I kept in the refrigerator. When my sister implored my mother to intercede, she replied, "Hopie's just not feeling well." Things reached a climax my junior year when I put myself on a starvation diet of tea with sugar and milk ... for over a month. As the pounds fell off, the boy I loved liked me better. My mother took me out to buy clothes. The message was clear: people loved me better when I was thin, so starving myself was the right thing to do. When that same boy ditched me, I gained eighty pounds. I was in college at that point, eating cafeteria food. Piles of cottage cheese and granola, healthy unless you ate them in quantities large enough to feed an army. Multiples of everything, from grilled cheese sandwiches to fried chicken and mashed potatoes. Anything to fill the void I felt inside.

Periodically, I'd crash diet, lose a pile of weight, find a new boyfriend, and be all right for a while. ... Until he left me and the void came back. I turned to food again. Food held me hostage. I was a drama major in college, even won awards for my roles, but I never was cast as the *ingenue*. I was too fat. I was always the mother or the mentally ill sister. Cinderella was not in my cards. I felt as if I were a prisoner in my body. I tried to convince myself I was healthy by running three miles a day. I tried to talk myself into gorgeous by picking up older men at the Copley Plaza and giving them the college girl experience of their fantasies. But when I had my senior pictures taken in our college arboretum, I was wearing a plaid, size sixteen dress. I felt frumpy and fat. So, what did I do? I took it off and posed nude, waist high in a stream. Needless to say, the photos never appeared in the college yearbook. I say these things neither to shock nor entertain. I tell them to demonstrate where food and body image took me.

People often think that it is only under the influence of alcohol and drugs that people get into trouble. Certainly, my experiences with alcohol and drugs took me into some pretty shady places. But so did food. I sometimes think my experience with food, and without it, has been like the fairytale of Hansel and Gretel. Taken in by the allure of gingerbread and sweets, they almost ended up roasted themselves. A misguided relationship with food is the reality of faulty plumbing. When I get sucked into thinking that food is something other than fuel for my body—when it becomes the replacement lover or the monstrous foe—I get into trouble. My pipes get clogged with literal and figurative poison that can't be simply flushed away.

༈

The most successful and significant step I have taken to recover from my food addiction is to practice balance in eating. There is nothing that I cannot eat. But everything I eat has consequences. For me, the most constructive diet program is one that has been around almost as long as I have. Weight Watchers is the only program I have ever used that has had lasting results. (Having said that, I have joined, lapsed, and rejoined several times.) The first time I joined WW was in 1988. I was engaged to be married and was carrying an extra thirty pounds. With the help of the program, I lost it. And then immediately became pregnant. Taking the advice from *What to Eat When You're Expecting* to heart, I gained sixty pounds with my son, and after he was born, I joined the program again. I lost all the weight. And I got pregnant again right away. At that point, my mother cautioned me from ever joining WW again, unless I wanted to birth a baseball team.

More recently, I came through a hard time—let go from work, husband dying of cancer—and I gained forty pounds. This time, my incentive was my daughter's wedding, and I lost those forty pounds in time to look presentable as the Mother of the Bride. All throughout my experience with the Weight Watchers program, I have learned to be less brutal on myself. I don't think of it as a diet; I think of it as a way of life. I have total freedom to eat whatever I choose to eat, however, I need to be honest and track what I am eating, not to punish myself but to allow myself the freedom to live in a healthy body that I love. Other programs may work for other people. Weight Watchers is the one that has worked for me.

Having said all that, I have recently cancelled my membership. I believe I have taken away all the knowledge I need about how to eat, what to eat; now, it is up to me to continue to practice the program without the restriction of having to stay within two pounds of my goal weight, a number that can be altered by drinking a cup of coffee or wearing a heavier top to the weigh-in.

And I no longer have to pay $14.95 a month.

༄

So what about the other substances we put in our mouths? Let's talk about drugs first. I never considered myself a drug addict. After all, I have never dropped acid, done a line of cocaine, or snorted or shot heroin. I'm almost a virgin when it comes to drug use. I made a commitment that I would steer clear of drugs to keep my parents happy. Of course, that didn't include smoking a little pot now and then. (It also didn't take into account the number of pills I took that were not prescribed to me.) Then there was that one time when my boyfriend gave me opium without telling me, just to see if he could break down my solid persona. I remember vaguely being woozy and then crashing into stacks of books—we were in the school library—and waking up at my friend Cynthia's house. It must have been bad, because my friends said they would never give me hard drugs again.

What I *did* use and abuse was alcohol. If I had a love/ hate relationship with food, I was married to alcohol. I don't really know when I had my first taste of alcohol. I have a vague memory of when I was about four years old, sipping from my grandfather's beer. The first real drink I was given was a gin and tonic one hot summer day in Maryland when I was twelve years old. My parents thought it would be a good idea.

Now that, as mentioned, I have been in recovery for many years, I often hear people tell how, in their early drinking years, they loved the taste of alcohol. I suppose I did. As a teenager, I used to sneak into the liquor cupboard and drink the booze out of the boxes of liquor-filled cherries my father was given for Christmas. In summer, when we went to Howard Johnson's for ice cream, I always chose rum raisin or coffee brandy. I was the type of drinker who mixed lemonade with her beer and her orange juice with vodka. I had a low tolerance for straight booze. The first time I had sake, at my high school graduation party, I went straight into a blackout. I remained a blackout drinker for the rest of my active drinking years.

My secret drinking guilt was over Holy Communion. I was on the altar guild and would often volunteer to assist at early morning services just so I just to taste that sweet wine in the morning. I was always a little jealous of my father, the priest, who got to finish off the remnants of what was left of the consecrated wine at the end of the service. I was sure he had put more in the chalice to bless than was necessary, just to get a hit. *I* wanted to get a hit anyway. Never mind that this was supposed to be Our Lord's blood, spilled for us. There were occasions when I just went straight for the jug in the sacristy.

In recovery circles, you hear a lot about the progression of the disease. At first, I guess you could say, alcohol "worked" for me. It gave me that pleasant, fuzzy buzz that let me escape my anxieties and fears. A glass of wine helped me loosen my grip on life, relax, and dream. But soon enough, one drink always led to another ... and another ... and another. Before I knew it, I was either puking my guts out in a trashcan or waking up next to a note from a stranger that read, "Thank you for the great time."

And those were the good moments.

It is sometimes hard for me to tell when alcoholism took over because of my bipolar disorder. In my teens and twenties, I was undiagnosed on either count. All I know is that I lived in a rapidly deteriorating cycle. Let me put it like this: years later, Thom and I took our three small children to Disney World in Orlando. One of the water slides at Hollywood Studios was called the "Royal Flush." You basically throw yourself into a vortex and are whirled around relentlessly until you drop with a splash into the pool below. That was my life as an alcoholic, only with each rotation, I became more depressed, more anxious, more paranoid, angrier, and more isolated than before. By the time I dropped into sobriety, I had given up on myself, my life, and everything. I totally surrendered, only because I simply could not fight any more.

When I first identified myself as an alcoholic, my family scoffed. My drinking friends did not believe me. Quite apart from the fact that I was threatening their own behavior, they couldn't understand how I, twenty-five at the time, wearing a size-four bikini, married to a Boston lawyer (my first husband), and embarking on a fabulous writing career, could be an alcoholic. After all, they rarely *saw* me drink. They never saw me drink because I hid my drinking. When my literary friends from Harvard or the District Attorney's office had parties, the champagne flowing like the Nile, I would hide out in the kitchen, doing dishes or preparing food to keep myself from taking that first drink. Because I didn't know what would happen if I did. Would I end up on some man's lap, trying to seduce him? Would I sit in the corner weeping? Would I put on a striptease and end up naked on the table, having cleared away the canapés and deviled eggs? (I am guilty of all of the above.) It was better, I figured, to suffer silently, leave early, and then go home and chug a bottle of wine or two before passing out on the bed. I knew I had a problem with alcohol, but I didn't know what to do about it. The thought never crossed my mind to simply not put alcohol into my mouth. What a crazy idea!

‿

I have made reference in this book already to the importance of complete surrender if we are going to change, and I will say it again. I could not get help with any of my faulty plumbing problems—booze, food, drugs, sex—until I was completely ready to surrender. Even as I say that word, I hear the Wicked Witch in *The Wizard of Oz* again, cackling as she spells out "Surrender, Dorothy" with her broomstick. I also see troops of bedraggled soldiers, filthy and exhausted, surrendering to the victorious side. These surrenders all smack of either imprisonment or loss of liberty, which is exactly how I felt when anyone suggested to me that I might want to change my eating habits or give up booze.

I always felt as if I were being given a life sentence, that all the joy in my life was being taken away, that nothing would be fun anymore.

I am here to tell you that the surrender of which I speak has had just the opposite effect. My addiction to food and booze wanted me to believe I was already having a good time. But I wasn't. I was fat (or so I thought), even when I wasn't fat, and totally uncomfortable in my body. When I drank, I was spiritually empty and I couldn't find peace anywhere I looked. Certainly not in the bottle. Those substances I took in through my mouth told me lies about my life that almost killed me.

I am so grateful for those moments when I have been able to sincerely say, "I need help" with something, or someone, outside of myself. People will tell you it is God's Grace that allows these moments to surface, and I don't deny that. I believe Grace has a lot to do with it. But it is also through the people who are put in our path that we are scooped up when we have gone astray. For me, in 1981, it was that young man from California who levelled with me. All I wanted was to have sex with him; what he gave me, instead, was sobriety—a far greater gift. Not too long ago, when I was so miserable about being heavy again, a friend walked into a meeting looking fabulous. "How?" I asked her. "Weight Watchers," she replied, and I followed her right back to the next meeting where I re-upped again. If we ask, sincerely ask, from the tips of our toes to the tiniest hairs on our heads, for God's help, we will get it. My experience is that help doesn't come in balls of lightning, but in chance meetings with friends and strangers. The solution to our problems lies in our connections with others and with a Higher Power.

But that is just the beginning. That is how I stopped using alcohol and food, drugs and sex. How I stay stopped is through a consistent practice of keeping track of my thoughts and actions; sharing those thoughts and actions honestly with another person or group; daily prayer and meditation; and last, but certainly not least, taking my prescribed medication daily. If I don't do these things, before I know it, I will be pouring the metaphorical paint thinner and bacon grease down my pipes, which will then become corroded and dysfunctional again. You would be surprised, and dismayed, if you knew how easy it is to veer off into negative behaviors.

To remind myself of just how easy it is to get off track, I keep a trio of Alexander Calder prints on a wall in my living room. They are reprints—my Aunt Christine brought back from Paris when she was studying art there long ago—of three acrobats on tightrope wire. Each one balances precariously on slender feet. My recovery from alcoholism and bipolar disorder is like these acrobats, dependent on acute mindfulness and attention to the moment. I must stay in the twenty-four hours of my day, doing just what is in front of me and practicing the same routine, if I am to have any success.

How many times in your life have you sworn off sweets only to find yourself chowing down on a giant box of chocolates? Or declared to the world that you're on the wagon for good this time, only to fall out of bed the next day with a terrific hangover? Or figured one little toke couldn't be all that bad … until you found yourself locked up in the local jail.

No one said this would be easy. But I have to tell you, it is worth it. There is nothing quite as lovely as the feeling I get when I am mindful of what I am ingesting. If I am responsible about what I eat, drink, and think— and what I do and do *not* put into my pipes—I can expect an abundantly happy life.

TOOLKIT #5

PRACTICE SELF-CARE. The tool that comes to mind when remodeling a life of addiction is actually more like a sheet that protects us from the onslaught of further decay. It is the Tarpaulin of Care. When we care for someone, which is really just a way of saying we love someone, we look out for their best interests. Sometimes our Care comes across as warm and fuzzy, which is generally well-received. But Care can be rough and painful too, like the Care that goes into an intervention. And intervention is not always welcomed by the afflicted one. Developing *self*-care is a skill that requires, above all, honesty as we scrutinize our actions, call ourselves out on unhealthy behaviors, and demand of ourselves that we change. Or, sometimes, we die. I have listed below those tools that have been necessary for me to rise from the ashes.

TAKE COURAGE. It takes a lot of courage to change. We humans tend to settle into habits, bad and good, and nothing but a spiritual explosion can move us from where we sit. Perhaps I should say "me," rather than "we." Inertia, that seductive shawl that wraps itself around my shoulders, kept me prisoner in my own misery for many years. Of course I didn't see it as misery. I just saw it as the way they were. I didn't know life could be any different. I was like Odysseus who, when trapped in Circe's den enjoying her lavish attention, finally remembered he had a wife and child waiting for him back in Ithaca. I was in the dark.

... Until the light broke through and someone offered me a hand to step out into a new way of being. It took all the courage I had to accept their offer of help, put down the booze and food, and try a different way of living. It wasn't easy. But it wasn't hard either, because deep down I was ready for change. Again, some people told me it was all God's Grace—and I certainly see God's hand in my years of recovery. But God doesn't merely strike us sober, clean, and abstinent until we take action, pick up the lightning rod, and begin to stimulate change by changing our actions.

I thank God every day for my sobriety and my healthy food choices. I go about my life making healthy choices: putting seltzer in my cup, not wine, and eating Greek yogurt and fruit for breakfast, not French toast dripping in syrup with a rasher of bacon.

Every day I choose to be a warrior for Hope.

Every day I choose Courage.

KEEP YOUR COMMITMENTS. One of my biggest pet peeves is people not keeping their commitments. Perhaps this is because, for so long, I didn't keep mine. In my using days, I disrespected those around me by showing up late for work, or brushing off appointments that became inconvenient without calling in advance. I have since come to appreciate the value of time—other people's and my own. I try not to make plans I won't be able to keep. I leave early to get where I am going so I don't keep people waiting. It just seems like common courtesy to me.

Keeping commitments to myself is just as important, maybe even more so. After all, if I can't count on myself, who can I count on? Fortunately, there are some very specific actions I can take to keep true to myself. With food, for years I kept a food log and that worked very well. There was even a time when I shared my food plan with a friend on a daily basis. That helped me stick to it. Today, I am a little looser than that. I find I can usually make good choices about what I eat, but if I find myself starting to slip off the rails, I will quickly pull out my notebook and start to track my meals again. This is true too if I find I am undereating. I need to keep my commitment to eating three healthy meals a day, with a snack in the afternoon. And to drinking at least eight cups of water daily. Exercise is much the same. I keep track of what I am doing, how much, and when. If I start to slide, I jump back in.

Commitment.

In the beginning, when I stopped drinking alcohol, I depended heavily on a friend to steer me through those early days of sobriety. I knew my intentions were good, but alcohol is a subtle foe. It calls the alcoholic like a siren song, so it is important to have tools in place to get you through the rough times. To demonstrate to my disease just how committed I was to sobriety, I went to meetings every day, sometimes two or three times per day, for well into three years. I stayed away from old friends or situations that could jeopardize my sobriety for the first year. I hung out with people who, like me, suffered from alcoholism but who also enjoyed volleyball, ballet, the beach, calligraphy, or eating out. We were all a happy band, and it made my commitment to sobriety easy. Over the years, and it has been many decades now, my routine has changed. But my commitment has not. I still attend meetings, work with other alcoholics, go to sober events, and enjoy my life. I am able to be around alcohol because my commitment is strong, but I don't like being around active drunks. Never have. Never will.

BE CONSISTENT. People shudder at the word "consistency," as if showing up every day and doing the same thing is somehow boring. I used to think so. I used to believe Emerson's statement that "A foolish consistency is the hobgoblin of little minds." Today I know I would never be sober, abstinent, and clean were it not for the consistency in my life. In fact, I would not be writing this book now, nor would I have published my other books, were it not for consistency. I would not be able to swim a mile easily or hike five miles without thinking were it not for consistency.

Great musicians show up every day to their instruments and practice, practice, practice so they can perform at Carnegie Hall. Athletes run sprints, do push-ups and sit-ups and leg lifts and curls, so they can make it to championships. You don't have to be spectacular to benefit from consistency. You just have to do it—whatever the "it" is that you have chosen to do. Take it one day at a time, do it one action at a time, and you will be a winner.

There is a misconception in recovery programs that it is somehow all right to relapse, to stop the commitment you have made to yourself. While relapse may happen in recovery, it is neither recommended nor necessary. I speak as one who has stayed sober since 1981 without a single relapse, despite all the shit life has thrown my way. People who relapse tell me it is hard to come back. Of course it is! You have chosen to bring to a screeching halt an engine that was throbbing with great momentum. Now try getting that engine stuck at the bottom of the hill to grind itself back into sobriety. For many, it is impossible and fatal.

Eating is the same way. While we can't take food totally out of our lives, we must be mindful of what we eat if we don't want to fall back into binging. As long as we keep our commitment to ourselves and honestly follow our programs, we can rest assured that life will continue to grow and change in positive ways.

"ONLY CONNECT." By its nature, addiction is a disease of isolation. For many years of my life, struggling either with alcohol or food, I kept myself separate from others. I attributed part of this to being an artist. After all, aren't the best artists those who sneak off into the woods and create masterpieces while living alone? (I guess there are probably one or two, like Thoreau and Ingmar Bergman, who chose solitude.) I chose to keep myself away from others out of fear that I would embarrass myself, shame that I wasn't good enough to be seen, and out of plain deceit. I wanted to do something I knew I shouldn't be doing. None of that worked very well for me. The truth is, we humans are social animals. We need one another to live, learn, and love during our lives.

My mother, an English teacher whom her students adored, had a poster on the wall of her classroom that read, *"Only connect!"* These words from E. M. Forster are so true. Connection has become the jewel in the crown of my sobriety. It is the thing that gives my life the most pleasure—next to writing. I value connection above almost anything else because when I am connecting with another person, really connecting, I am transported out of my very limited self and brought into a whole new world of compassion and love.

Over the decades, I have met thousands of people who have all played very important parts in my life, not just in my sobriety and abstinence. Everyone—from Dorothy Clifton, my godmother, who taught me unconditional love; to Dolores Ambrister, my stern Latin teacher and choral director who modeled for me persistence and passion; to Tom Cole, my writing mentor who gave me confidence; and Thom Andersen, my dear husband who demonstrates daily the value of humor and compassion—*everyone,* plus so many more, have added a drop of positive energy into my very deep bucket so that it is now filled to the brim with hope. I would not have stayed sober without the women and men who were there to support me. I would not have survived the devastation of my parents' deaths and my own manic meltdown had it not been for those who stood beside me. I could not have made it through my husband's cancer and my own depression if I had not connected with others.

Connection is a vital tool in recovery, in life. And yet, dialing the phone can feel like such a hard thing to do. If it is hard for you to connect at first, start small. Talk to the cashier at the checkout. Wave at the neighbor you have never met. Call a friend and ask them about themselves. People always want to talk about themselves. Each time you connect, you will feel a little better about yourself. Gradually, connecting will become second nature. You will realize that you actually do care about yourself and others!

CHAPTER 6
Raise The Roof

I have always loved the word "raise." Spelled this way, to raise means to lift up, as in a barn raising, in which neighbors help one another to create a new dwelling on their farm. We raise our children with love, in hopes that they will become caring, thoughtful adults who will then nurture more caring, thoughtful young people of their own. We are blessed at work with monetary raises that demonstrate our employers' confidence in us and appreciation for our efforts. We raise our voices in protest when things need to be changed. And in song when we show our gratitude. And, in terms of a house, to raise the roof means to give shelter and safety from the outside.

The opposite of all this is to *raze*. It sounds the same but means something entirely different. To raze a building is to level it, destroy it completely. We can raze people's hopes and dreams, and our own, when we do not pay attention to what we are doing.

Doing is the operative word. So I want to talk to you in this chapter about exactly what it is we do to "keep a roof over our heads," our jobs, and how sometimes—for me anyway—the desire to make money has been the very thing that razed my self-esteem and kept me from knowing and loving who I really am.

⌁

I know I am skating on thin ice here. I hear my critics say that I have been in a marriage for thirty-plus years, I'm basically supported by my husband's salary, and I've been living on Social Security Disability since 2000, so what do I know about supporting myself? The first thing I would like to point out is that having a job, no matter how small or how grand, has always been necessary for me, a way of making myself feel "valuable." Frankly, however, that is a belief I have come to know as one of the most pernicious lies I ever fell for. I *am* valuable, we are all valuable, with or without a paycheck. But in our society, we have been led to believe that the more money you make, the more valuable you are. So, the homeless, unemployed and stay-at-home moms are discounted, public servants are belittled, and dishonest businessmen are held in high regard. Don't get me started.

I have a rather interesting work history, and an even more bizarre relationship with money. It all began a long time ago.

ᴣ

When I was a preteen, I sought out babysitting jobs and random chores so I could save money. I didn't know what I was saving for. There was no Barbie doll I wanted, nor a pair of nice skates; I just wanted the security of having money in my account. I loved going to the bank with my little book and watching the numbers add up—into the thousands by the time I graduated from high school. And then, in one fell swoop, it all disappeared.

Since I had skipped the seventh grade and would be graduating early, my parents insisted I take a year abroad after high school, in part to get away from my boyfriend whose baby I wanted to have. At fifteen, that didn't sound like a good idea to them. So off I went to Europe where I traveled to the islands of Greece, the streets of Paris, the villages of Italy, and more. It was all fun, I have to admit, until that day in Geneva, Switzerland, when I ran flat out of money and had to call home. Years' worth of savings had vanished in just nine months. And in the end, no baby. Just memories and some regrets.

This began years of struggling with money. I attended an Ivy League college as a scholarship student. I was surrounded by rich girls who flew off to the islands for holidays and carried thousand-dollar handbags. They drove fancy cars—BMWs, Audis, Porsches—while my family could only afford one car for the four of us left at home. So, I walked to my job cleaning houses for the faculty, or working in the cheese store in town, or serving beer at the college student union. I made enough to pay for shampoo and tampons, but I felt bitter and low.

When I graduated from college with a degree in theatre studies and English, I wasn't fit for much employment. I was scared I would never be able to support myself, so I moved in with a man twenty-five years my senior, with whom I had been in some plays in college. He made a decent salary as a lawyer. There is a word for that kind of desperation, I know. But just to show how independent and righteous I was, I landed a job teaching speed reading at a private school in New England, which I continued until, one day, the lawyer showed up at my dorm with a diamond ring and a bottle of champagne.

Our marriage lasted four years, during which my drinking and behavior became totally out of control. I did manage, in that time, to convince Harvard University to hire me as the Director of Public Relations for the Arnold Arboretum. This was a job for which I was entirely unqualified, and I went every day for a year wearing pretty outfits and dreading what would come up at work that I didn't know how to handle. At that time in both my drinking and my youth, I did not know how to ask for help. So, one day, I just quit.

I convinced myself it was time to be a writer. That, and a bottle of Scotch, got me nowhere. Actually, that's not true. In three months' time, using Syd Fields' book *Screenplay* as a guide, I wrote a screenplay that almost sold. I had a story published and a poem. I studied with famous poets and authors, like Derek Walcott, Andre Dubus, and Tom Cole. For about two years, it all looked good, sounded good, but I was making no money and the drinking was progressing.

꒰

Fast forward to 1981. By now, that date should ring a bell with you. That summer, I was working as a teaching assistant for George Garrett alongside Madison Smartt Bell. I remember that was the summer George discovered Carolyn Chute, author of *The Beans of Egypt, Maine.* Listening to Carolyn read, I felt like a fraud. My writing stank. All I could do was drink—until a kind soul took me to a twelve-step meeting and told me the truth about myself: I was an alcoholic.

That discovery led to a complete change in my life and my attitude about work and money. Suddenly, the most important thing was not that I become an Oscar-winning screenwriter. The most important thing was that I stay sober, gain humility, and help my fellows. After several vain attempts at employment—working at a fruit and vegetable market, selling things at Crate and Barrel, and nannying a one-year-old girl—I dragged myself back to Harvard and got a job as a secretary in the Freshman Dean's Office. I moved out from living with my first husband (soon to be ex) into a rent-controlled apartment. I walked to work and meetings and everywhere else for three years. My life simplified. I was so grateful for that menial job because it paid my bills, kept me humble, and allowed me time to heal.

Of course, I got restless. I was not satisfied with the little I had and went in search of more.

My answer came one autumn afternoon in 1983 when I was sitting by the shores of Lake Waban in Wellesley, Massachusetts, reading Dante Alighieri's *The Divine Comedy*. I realized I wanted to study that great work in depth because it spoke to me so personally about my own shortcomings. I researched where such study might take place and found I could study *The Divine Comedy* and obtain a Masters in Divinity from Yale Divinity School, while simultaneously receiving a teaching certificate in English from the college. I would be able to indulge my desire to learn as well as obtain credentials for a new career. This seemed like the voice of Heaven. So, killing two birds with one stone, I took myself off to Yale to get a Masters ... and went $40,000 in debt.

When I graduated, I accepted my first job as a teacher, at the age of thirty-one, making just $18,000 per year. Try living in Princeton, New Jersey on $18,000 a year. I had to find a roommate. I ended up sharing a house with one of the middle school science teachers, a biking enthusiast with whom I did not get along. She was just as stubborn and selfish as I was. I left that situation full of resentment and took on a position as a housekeeper for a wealthy couple from New York City who kept a "farm" outside of town. I cleaned for them in exchange for living rent-free at the house. This allowed me, on my teacher's salary, to make ends meet. At that time, I met and began dating my soon-to-be second husband. Due to circumstances beyond anyone's control—the wife suffered from complications during pregnancy and was ordered to stay in bed in the city—Thom and I found ourselves living alone in this beautiful house with a pool and enough seclusion to indulge in our budding love affair. We lived like this for about six months or so, until the couple returned and replaced me with another woman. But that is a whole other topic. Meanwhile, I tried to convince myself that teaching was my noble calling, but then I looked around at all the rich kids I taught and their rich parents—everyone reeking of snobbery and entitlement, including myself—and I wanted out.

☙

My "out" came when I got pregnant. My days of motherhood had begun. Between 1990 and 1994, we had three beautiful, healthy children. Those were confusing years for me. When my son, our first born, came along, I was all too ready to turn to mothering full-time, but I soon became bored with the monotony of small things. I didn't feel like I fit in with the other mothers in our play group. My intellectual pride told me that being a mother twenty-four seven was somehow "below" me. It wasn't the work I was cut out for, and besides, it didn't pay.

So, I put my son in daycare and went back to teaching, this time at a community college, part-time. I was bringing in money, stroking my ego, and spending just enough time with my son to feel useful. I felt I had achieved a balance. I had just hit my stride and was promoted to full-time at the college, when I got pregnant again. Life became more complicated still when, that November, while I was about five months along, my mother was killed in an automobile accident. I threw myself into my work to mask my feelings, but they eventually seeped out anyway in the form of postpartum depression. I began my first experience with medication. I was put on fluoxetine—Prozac—which was at that time presumed to be a cure-all for everything. It did nothing for me. That spring, I put my six-week-old infant into child care with her brother, convinced that my teaching was more important than the stress my absence put on my children, my family. I had a purpose. I was bringing in money. What could be wrong with that?

ᾱ

Two years later, I gave up that job because we had our third child. It would be more than I could bring home to keep them all in child care. For the next four years, I played stay-at-home mom, a job totally underappreciated and misunderstood by anyone who hasn't been there, done that. Honestly, those years are pretty much a blur. I just remember the overall woozy feeling I had all the time from lack of sleep and constant attention paid to little ones whose sole purpose in life seemed to be to drive me to distraction. I was—am—such a selfish person that showering all that affection and attention on them left me wanting to scream, "What about me?" at the end of every day. They were not interested in my theories about Dante's *Inferno*. They couldn't care less if I knew all of Emily Dickinson's poems by heart. They wanted what they wanted when they wanted it, or they would cry and fight and tear things up. Who knew that such small, adorable creatures could be such giant pains in the ass?

When my youngest was three, I applied for and got a job at the local seminary as a writer and editor. It seemed like a job made in heaven. The older two were in school. The baby had child care paid for as a perk of working, and I was back in the land of the living, carrying on adult conversations and bringing home good money. Until, in 1997, my dad died of prostate cancer and my life fell apart. I may have had symptoms of bipolar disorder before, but now the illness took over full force.

This is the hardest thing for me to write about because I hurt so many people at this time, myself included, all due to mental illness. When my father died, I went to my parish priest for grief counseling. He was totally understanding and could see through the transference that I was imposing on him. I don't believe he had any idea that I had bipolar disorder, no one did then, but he could tell something was up and he kept his respectful, professional distance while being supportive. All this time, I was drawing further away from my husband, blaming him for things over which he had no control, like the fact that we had missed being with my father as he passed.

When my parish priest went on vacation, I confided in another priest at the seminary where I worked, but he was not so honorable. He took advantage of my fragile state and, soon enough, we were meeting during our lunch hour where we carried on an affair for some months during the spring and summer. But this was no normal affair. This was mental illness at its height. This was me believing I truly loved this man, that I would leave my children for him, that I would give up everything for him. This was me imagining him as Denzel Washington or Sidney Poitier, when truly he was just a scrawny little man who was cheating on his very nice wife while I cheated on my wonderful husband.

By August, when Princess Diana was killed, I had burned out. The mania was over and had turned to depression. We cut off relations and life went on. ... Until December, when my husband found a journal in which I had written about the events of that spring and summer, and he then went into a depression of his own. This led him to seek solace from another woman—a fact that I could not bear—and I threatened to take my own life. So, that was when he had me institutionalized. It was such a horrible period in our lives.

I ended up with a fractured marriage, in a psychiatric hospital, painting ceramic figures with my three small children who cried when our visits ended. I cried too. Still, there was a silver lining. Were it not for that breakdown, I might never have been diagnosed as bipolar and set on the path to manage that terrible disease.

But let's not sugarcoat it. That episode, that affair, cost me a myriad of relationships. I lost credibility and support in my twelve-step community because, frankly, people who are sober just aren't supposed to act like that. No matter how much I tried to convince myself that I was sick, in the throes of mental illness at the time, I could not get away from the guilt and remorse that I felt. My infidelity and mental illness devastated my husband, who already suffered from PTSD prior to the event. He could not function at work to the point that he was let go. And I could not stay in my job with the judgement I was receiving there.

We eventually sold our house in New Jersey and moved to Michigan, dragging our children away from their friends and stability. This was especially hard on my oldest son, who had witnessed the arguments between Thom and me and took all this anguish to heart. My sisters judged me, though they were going through their own reactions to Dad's death. Thom, the kids, and I lived in exile for years after. Life blew up. Nuclear. And all because I had—and did not understand—bipolar disorder.

If I can help anyone, anywhere, see something of this in themselves so they can seek help before the explosion, all that occurred will not have been for naught.

Bipolar disorder. I had my answer for questions I had been asking myself all my life. Suddenly, my actions made perfect sense. All those ups and downs; the inability to hold a job after landing an impossibly good one; the grandiosity of thinking that my employment was oh, so important while questioning to my core the ability to handle even the smallest job. My giant manic episode had robbed me of belief in myself, belief that I could do anything or be anyone without hurting everyone around me.

For years afterwards, I stayed at home, my tail between my legs, feeling guilty and ashamed over something beyond my control. I got on disability, which allowed me to stay home, and I appreciated that while at the same time resenting it. Disability meant I couldn't go for a prestigious job to make me feel better, more important. It kept me tethered to my home. I made stabs at part-time jobs—ghostwriting for a while, teaching a course or two at community colleges, tutoring—but those jobs never gave me the same rush as the full-time, bigger money deals that had given me titles and turned me into someone important, rather than the loser I deeply believed I was.

రి

By 2008, we had moved to North Carolina. It had been almost ten years since the last manic episode. I was in a good doctor's care, and the kids were all nearly grown. I decided—we decided, actually—that we could use the money, and I went back to work, teaching high school full-time. This is what I had gone to graduate school for: to reach young minds and shape them into something positive and new. Instead, mine was the only mind that was bent.

Teaching at our local public high school was a thankless task. I only stayed as long as I did because, at that point, my husband was sick and I was afraid he was going to die. But every day for me was an exercise in practicing hope, vigorously challenging myself to stay afloat although I felt like I was drowning. The hardest part of that job was my belief that I didn't have any other option. I was certified to teach English at the high-school level. That was it. I believed I had no other skills, nowhere else I could turn. I felt totally boxed in. All the while, my quality of life was going downhill. I was forty pounds overweight, not sleeping well, not being intimate with my spouse, and I had no real friends. All I did was work and spin my wheels in the mud.

And then they decided not to renew my contract.

You know the rest of my work history. In 2013, I became caretaker for my sick husband. In 2015, he almost died. When he didn't, I decided to do something with my life that felt right for me, and that I could live with. I started to write. Writing, thus far, has not exactly paid well—at least not monetarily—but other types of currency do exist.

Doing what I love has paid off in the currency of compassion. I am far nicer to everyone around me than I ever was in any of my other jobs. My new lifestyle has, also, paid me handsomely in time. I have time to prepare and eat healthy meals, to exercise, to answer calls, to rest, to sleep. I no longer believe I am a loser or a fraud. On the contrary, I feel for the first time in my work life that I am being true to myself. Because of this, I have heaps of energy and loads of inspiration. But not in a manic way. Now that I am allowing myself to raise the roof I really want to have over my head, I find I am more able to be patient and loving toward others. Feeling so connected to my true calling creates a magic cocoon around me. I don't feel threatened by other peoples' successes, their wealth, their celebrity any longer. I know I am on the right path for me and that whatever is supposed to unfold for me in this life will unfold if I just stick to this path and follow my joy.

I hear the scoffers saying "Easy for you. You have your husband and your Social Security Disability." To these folks I would say, "How is your job working for you? Are you happy? Are you healthy?" Rationalization is the enemy of change.

When I was working in the high school, miserable and sick in spirit, I rationalized that I had to be there because we needed the money and it was all I could do. Both claims proved to be erroneous. What I know about having money is that if I have it, I spend it. It doesn't matter if it is $60,000 or sixty cents. So why should I stay in a job that is torturing my soul if the money I make is just going to disappear as soon as it comes in.

In the Lord's Prayer, we pray, "Give us this day our daily bread." When the Israelites were wandering in the desert, God provided enough manna for them each day to get through to the next. That's what I think money is really about, in the best sense. Simply getting us through to the next day.

In my *Hopenomics*, as my husband calls them, God provides. I always have—we always have—enough to meet life's demands. We don't have excess. We don't buy expensive cars, but our vehicles run just fine. Tomorrow we both have the day off and we are going to take a five-mile hike beside the lake at a park we have never been to before. When my demands are not outrageous, when my expectations aren't so lopsided they could capsize a boat, when I simply ask for my daily bread, God gives it to me. It's been that way forever.

One of the most recent ways that God has intervened to help us take responsibility for our finances is to introduce us to Dave Ramsey's *The Total Money Makeover*. I was first introduced to this program back in Michigan, fifteen years ago, but I was not ready to hear the truth. In more recent months, our oldest daughter, knowing how we struggle with money, approached us about the program she and her new husband had adopted. It was Dave Ramsey's *The Total Money Makeover*. This time, the news fell on willing ears, and we have been practicing his program since January 2020, making swift headway and feeling much more confident about the roof over our heads.

From inspirational books to so many other things—trips, flowers, clothes, houses, family—the Universe has provided for me in lovely ways. But only when I have moved out of the way and let God do God's thing. I have it all wrong if I am wrapped up in knots, struggling with a job I hate, and working just because I think said job is going to give me the things that make me happy. Once I uncoil from those twisted lies that keep me prisoner in my misery, I can begin to experience the real joy that comes when I am living the right life for me.

So, let us raze the roof of Responsibility, Maturity, and Overall Grumpiness and raise, instead, a new roof that lets the light of our Spirits shine through. Let go of the "shoulds" and "oughts" that have defined you, and take a leap into the arms of a loving Universe whose only hope for you is Joy!

TOOLKIT #6

FOLLOW. The most important tool I have used in my journey toward finding my true calling is to follow. That may seem strange, I know, in this society where we are all encouraged to be leaders and forge the way. But for me, holding life in my hands as if it is some kind of magic rope, leading me to where I need to go has been so helpful for me. I heard, when I was just a young girl, the message relayed in George MacDonald's tale *The Golden Key*. This message stated that in order to be happy, we must follow our calling. As a young girl, I felt *my* calling was pretty clear: I was born to be an actress. I held tightly to that rope. As a sophomore in high school, I tried to convince my parents to send me to the North Carolina School of the Arts. They refused and, instead, sent me abroad for a year.

Then, when I was told I would be attending an Ivy League college instead of an arts school, I majored in theatre studies. My second year there, I was invited to join a summer theatre program in Vermont, the Green Mountain Guild. My parents told me no, we didn't have the money. It was probably a good thing, as I am told Meryl Streep, an inspired actress even then, performed there that summer, and I am sure I would have perished in her glorious light. I applied to Yale School of Drama for graduate school and was rejected. You would have thought by now I might have caught on that this career path was not for me.

So, if acting was not to be my calling, what was? Holding on to that invisible line and following what my heart told me, I was led into writing. But I got it all wrong. I thought that writing was about becoming a Famous Author, about making money and winning awards. So, I fueled my writing with alcohol, destroying any true creativity I might have had. And when I got sober, I stopped writing for many years. By keeping my journal and penning little poems for myself, I kept my hand in my craft. I became a ghostwriter, working on several books, and forayed into screenwriting, writing a half dozen screenplays. I kept my hand on the line, but there was always this sense that I was a fraud. I was not a real writer. Still, I followed my heart, in spite of my reservations, as I pursued careers as a teacher, a publicist, and then an editor. What I did not know during all that time, but know now, is that I was a writer all along. I just wasn't able to see my calling as something separate from making money. I was like the teacher who tells the budding artist to stay inside the lines; in order to follow my calling, I needed to let go of unrealistic expectations and just have fun.

ASK. So, how do you know what your true calling is? Ask. And I don't mean go get a Myers/Briggs Personality Test. I mean ask the Universe. Pose the questions: Who am I? Ask yourself, as Mary Oliver does in her poem "The Summer Day," "Tell me, what is it you plan to do / with your one wild and precious life?"[14] This is really a conversation you must carry on with the Universe and yourself under a pink moon, or sitting quietly in a room where the loudest sound is the dust motes showering. This is meditation. This is magic. And when you start to feel an answer, pick up the line and follow it. Or maybe you won't have an answer right away. Just be open for clues—the little things that get you excited and bring you joy. I can't tell you where your happiness will come from. Only you will know that. But I can tell you that when I started responding to the inklings that encouraged me to write again, this time without expectations, my world opened up. First, I had to ask.

LEARN. In my "previous life" as I like to call it, I thought I needed to know what a book said before I read it. I finished people's sentences for them because I knew what they should say. It was very important to me to have all the answers, to make up for the fact that I felt so insecure—and at the same time, superior—inside. This trait got in the way of sending my writing out or sharing it, because as long as the work was on my desk at home, it could be the great American novel or the Pulitzer Prize-winning poem. As I sat in my cocoon, buffered from judgement and criticism, I could entertain any fantasy I wanted. But that was just it: they were fantasies.

One of the greatest gifts I have been given at this stage of my life is the ability to learn. Who says you can't teach an old dog new tricks? I learn plenty and enjoy every new morsel I ingest. Where once I was averse to joining a writing workshop, out of pride and fear, I now look for occasions during which I can share my work and have it critiqued. My greatest ally is my editor, who combs over my pages and offers useful suggestions while taking the red pen to paper. My books are always better because of her.

Learning isn't just about becoming better at your job; it's also about becoming better at your life. In order to be better at what I do, I have had to learn to be both disciplined and flexible. I set myself a time to write in the mornings, but if my husband needs to have a conversation with me or the dogs need to be fed, I can step aside from what I am doing and take a few minutes to be nice. The page will wait, and I have learned to trust that I can pick up where I left off. I know I can work at most any time of day, although I prefer the quiet of the early hours. I am a lot more resilient than I once thought I was. We each need to learn, not only about the mechanics of what we do but about the mystery of who we are.

SHADOW. Shadowing is a very useful tool in discovering what your true calling is and where you want to be. I have two daughters. Both are in the dental field. As they sought their current positions, they each shadowed potential employers to see where they might best fit. As a result, both have ended up in positions for which they are well suited, with colleagues they enjoy.

This seems so sensible to me. Not shadowing is like ordering clothes online. You never know what they are really going to look like or how they are going to fit. Shadowing puts you smack in the center of a situation and allows your inner voice to speak to you about the appropriateness, or not, of the position. Of course, this is assuming you listen to your inner voice! Most professional roles encourage shadowing. Companies want their employees to be happy, because a happy employee is a productive employee. To young people, I would say: try out as many jobs as interest you. Don't just go for the ones that you think are sensible. Entertain a myriad of possibilities. You never know what is lurking in the shadows!

RESPOND. Once you have established what your calling is (determine whether you can support yourself with that one career or need a supplemental job as well) and have set out to learn more about the positions, you are ready to respond. There is a big difference between reacting and responding.

I have a friend who has been going through a rather intensive job search. She is at a point now where she is feeling the crunch to take a position. She has been offered a job, but the job is more demanding than she would like and does not offer the compensation she deserves. Still, she is enthusiastic about the company's program and would enjoy the work environment. Furthermore, she is waiting to hear from another company about an opportunity, one that she deems almost perfect. What should she do? While some might say a bird in the hand is worth two in the bush, I say wait. Do not jump into accepting an offer just because you are afraid that another one might not come along. If there are red flags—and there are several in my friend's first offer—don't leap. It would be dissatisfying to leap, out of haste, into a role that doesn't feel right for you.

I have leapt into situations that ended up costing me wasted years and chunks of my soul. Those leaps were choices I would regret today had I not left all that behind. People have many different reasons for accepting jobs that may not be right for them. Personally, I took "imperfect" jobs for one of two reasons: either my pride told me I was ready to handle them, or my fear told me I needed the money. Seldom were my searches directed by a desire to help others, although I told myself they were. And yet, isn't this the true purpose of life? To be of service to others? Isn't service where our true happiness and purpose come from? Doing the thing we love to do, are called to do, in the service of others seems to be the perfect prescription for joy.

The best way I can help others is to be true to myself, and do the things I am called to do. For me, those callings are to work in a bookstore and write. Money isn't everything. Certainly, we need enough to live—pay rent and bills, eat. But I have found that when we do the things we are called to do, the Universe really does take care of the rest.

So, be careful what you choose. When you do choose to work, make sure you are *responding* and not reacting to the offer.

BE TEACHABLE. Now that you have chosen your employment, you need to *believe* it is the right thing for you at the time. There are going to be great days ahead in your job, but there will always be some challenging ones too. You will feel happy with or neutral about most of your colleagues, but inevitably there will be one or two who rub you the wrong way. This is life. You don't need to change your job or change the other people. Believe that the Universe has placed you in this situation so you can learn something about yourself.

I have a co-worker at the bookstore who really got on my nerves at first. She was so bossy, such a know-it-all. As previously mentioned, I grumbled about her to my husband, building up a resentment in my soul. Then, while reading Pema Chödrön one morning, I thought to myself, "What kind of spirituality do I have if I am harboring these ill feelings?" So, I started to pray for her. Not a lot. I didn't want to go overboard. But occasionally I would send out little prayers for her happiness. Wouldn't you know it, my prayers and little acts of kindness toward her changed everything. This woman who once seemed bossy and like a know-it-all, now seems experienced and helpful. Her rough edges have softened.

... Okay, so I know *my* rough edges are the ones that have softened; she never was the harridan I made her, that was my filter. When I told her I would be taking a sabbatical to write two new books, she was genuinely sorry to see me go but promised she would try to make it to my upcoming launch. We parted as friends. This kind of transformation always makes me believe in the goodness of the Universe. If I can just align myself with what is right, my life is so much smoother.

CHAPTER 7
The Master Suite

One of my friends from water aerobics, a widow from New Jersey, has decided to sell her old house and build a new one on the lake. She showed me the plans of her new home as we ate chicken salad sandwiches in her kitchen one afternoon.

Looking around her old house, I wondered why she was leaving. Her "old" house—maybe twenty years old—is in pristine condition, light and airy, with a beautifully landscaped backyard, mature trees, and a sunroom that stretches clear across the back of her property. I was curious about her resolve to go through the hassle of buying, selling, packing, and moving, but, as she explained to me, it was time to let go of her two-story home that held so many memories of her late husband. She was ready to move on to something new—not smaller, just shorter—that was more aligned with her present life.

While my friend is eager to move into her new, shorter home, there is one thing she will not surrender: her master suite. The master suite is the anchor that holds the new house plans together. In fact, the master suite in her lake house will be larger and more "user friendly" than the one inland ever was. It will not only comprise a nineteen-by-nineteen-foot bedroom with lake views, it will also boast an almost equally large bathroom, an enormous clothes closet, and an adjoining laundry room so that she can, as she says, "just slip out of what I am wearing and throw it in the wash." She has put a lot of thought into what she wants in a master suite, and the one she has designed suits her just fine.

༄

When we look at our lives and our recovery, we need to focus that same diligent attention on our own "master *suite*," the core of our being. Home base, if you will. Or, in other words, what we protect with our self-care. Earlier, I illustrated how the words 'raise' and 'raze' are homonyms representing opposite ideas. In this case, I'll stretch a little futher and suggest that 'suite' and 'sweet' share a similar relationship. My master suite, the place which grounds me in my life, is the sweet spot that my self-care nurtures. It is the opposite of that saccharin or false sweetness that comes from pretending I am taking care of myself by, for example, starving myself or perpetuating an unhealthy relationship. Pretend long enough, and you will have forgotten how to love yourself. But loving myself *is* the most important thing

I can do today. I must care for my master suite, not just master the "sweet" stuff.

I spent years, decades even, in recovery from alcoholism and bipolar disorder, rehashing the guilt and remorse I felt over my selfish and often cruel behavior. I have since learned that rehashing is just another form of selfishness. My mother used to say that guilt was a four-letter word. And I believe that. Beating myself up with guilt over past behavior kept me stuck and, like tires stuck in the mud, I just spun around. The wonderful thing about the twelve steps is that they enable the alcoholic to let go of the past, take responsibility for it, make amends and move on. I had a hard time doing that around my alcoholism and bipolar disorder because, fundamentally, I hadn't taken the first step yet: admitting that I was powerless over my diseases and that life had become unmanageable.[15] Until I firmly surrendered to the reality that I was—am—truly an ill person, I could not get well.

If insanity is doing the same thing over and over and expecting different results, wallowing in self-pity was the very thing that kept me crazy.

౨

I can also be kept "crazy" by cloaking my insanity in phony "sweetness," convincing myself and others that my charity toward others should supersede my tending to my own life. In the past, I sometimes tried to hide from my defects of character by fixing others' situations or taking care of their needs. In truth, this was a very selfish act. I needed to let people, whomever they were, follow their own paths, discover their own ways, not hover over them like some dysfunctional angel. I needed to set boundaries and stay inside them, and not use others' difficulties to make me feel better about myself.

So, how well do we disguise our selfishness in "selfless" acts? I can do a million great and charitable things in a year, but if underneath that charity is seething envy or resentment, if I am exhausted by all my good works, if I am constantly looking for praise and approval, then I might as well not have done anything at all. People can sense a phony. Then again, sometimes we get so wrapped up in our own denial that we are unable to see the truth about ourselves. The truth is: I need to truly love myself before I can love anyone else.

I have butted heads with others along my recovery path when I say that self-love is the most important thing I can do on a daily basis. Down here where I live, in the Bible Belt, there is an unwritten law that you must put others first. Be the first one with the sweet-potato casserole after surgery. Be the leader who pulls together a meal train for a new mom who has just had a baby, or a person suffering from illness. Take children into your home to give their mother a rest. Offer to drive an elderly couple to the airport. Don't get me wrong, these are all good things as long as they are actions taken in love and not performed as a sense of duty. "I *should* do X" we often hear ourselves saying. A wise man once said to me, "Don't should on yourself."

If the action I take is going to cause me or my family hardship or resentment, then I really need to check my motives. Why am I insisting on chairing that committee or volunteering for that guild at church? Is it my ego? My pride? Or do I genuinely want to be of service? Does the idea of helping bring me joy? These are questions I need to ask myself. One of the things I have learned about serving others is that sometimes I am not the right one for the job. Oftentimes there are plenty of people who can fill the position better than I can, and who may *need* to fill the position more than I do. It is important that I remember just how important I am: BIG and small, simultaneously, as Buddhist teacher and nun, Pema Chödrön, would say. Or in twelve-step lingo, I need to stay "right-sized."

ॐ

Back to self-love: in his second commandment, Jesus said, "Love thy neighbor as thyself." Now I am more spiritual than I am religious, but I get that. How can I possibly love anyone else if I am such a harsh judge of my own behavior, and if I am the "critical parent" who is always finding fault with what I do and who I am?

Self-love and self-care are not luxuries. They are not selfish indulgences. They are absolutely necessary if I am going to engage in relationships that are healthy and vibrant. I like to think of my self-care as my master suite—my rooms where I live, sleep, love, bathe, dress, where I spend at least eight hours a day. At least once a day, I check myself out in the mirror to see if I still am who I think I am. Self-care is all about this room.

༈

When I was a young child, I shared a room with my sisters. We lived on the first floor of a dormitory at the private school where my father was the chaplain. There was not much room for our family of eight. At that time, my life was undifferentiated from my siblings'. I was seen as just one of the six girls. Shoved together in a small space, we were lumped together in our identities. When space became available, the school recognized my parents' dilemma and moved us up the hill to the old headmaster's house. I insisted on—fought tooth and nail for—having my own room. I knew even back then, in elementary school, how important it was for me to have my own space. All that was available was a storage closet, or so I remembered it. (I have since been corrected and informed that it was a desirable space, though small, with its own bathroom.) Nevertheless, to *me* it was a storage closet. I lived there for the short time our family remained in Connecticut, and I hated that space. It was dark and scary. There was a huge window that looked out on the hill behind the house, and I was sure some bad man would come out of the woods and murder me—or worse. Every night, I would get out of bed and race the length of the carpeted hall to my parents' bedroom where I would then sleep either with them or on the floor.

When we moved to Maryland, where my father had been given a school of his own to run, we had a huge plantation home with bedrooms enough for everyone, including Grandma, who had come to stay, as well as the three "boarders"—girls who attended my father's school and lived with us for several years. In those years, from fourth to ninth grade, I was shuffled from one bedroom to another, probably at my own insistence. Whatever the reason, life was chaotic and unsettled as the landscape of the house kept changing. Grandma came and went, the boarder girls moved out, sisters got married and went off to college, as I played out my high school years.

At this time, I finally landed in a little room on the third floor, which I loved. It had two window seats, where I sat, gazing out over the woods, the horse pastures, and the campus. I decorated everything in yellow and orange, from bedspread to stools. The room was my happy place in an otherwise troubled time. My own little "master suite" was my sanctuary where I could breathe and be me.

Virginia Woolf knew the importance of having a room of one's own. I have always treasured my privacy and my sacred space. Today, I have a house that I love, but more importantly, I have my own room that I adore. Filled with my treasured books, Christmas lights, and a comfy armchair, my room is where I read, write, meditate, and dream, usually with our beagle, Quinn, on my lap. But I digress.

After I graduated from high school, my parents sent me abroad to study in England for a year. For the first few weeks, I roomed with two girls, one of them being the only black girl in the school. One day when she and I were on a walk, she ran off and didn't come back. She had felt so confined, imprisoned, isolated. And she had been. That day when she left me at the crossroads, she threatened to kill me if I said anything. I ratted her out anyway, to the headmistress, immediately upon returning to school. I was blamed for her actions and sent to live in the "bad girls'" house, where we were treated like criminals for petty crimes. The girls who lived there had been caught smoking or meeting with boys outside the campus on the weekends. They were the belligerent ones who refused to wear their school ties or whose parents had sent them to a boarding school because they couldn't cope with the teens. These girls were a colorful lot, and I enjoyed being with this band of rabble rousers, almost more than the porcelain-like prefects back in the main house.

The second trimester, I was allowed back into the main house. My new roommates smuggled gin into our room and blew cigarette smoke out of the skylight in the bathroom. But all I wanted was some peace and quiet, danger free. I didn't want to get in trouble again. I finally got that peace during my final trimester, when I had earned enough trust to be given a single room overlooking the courtyard. To live alone was dreamy. I didn't have to listen to other people's music or complaints. I was alone and able to weep when I felt homesick—not for my family but for my boyfriend who wrote me cryptic notes a couple of times. "Come home a great lady." What did that mean? I was 3,000 miles away and that was all he could say? I should have known he had found someone else. I couldn't wait to leave and return home. And as for my former roommate? She never did return to school, as far as I was aware.

But when I returned, my family had moved to a small house in Vermont, big enough for only a third of the family. I don't know if it was the fact that I didn't have any place to call my own, or that the love of my life had left me for another girl, or that my drinking was becoming out of control, but those were terrible years, 1973 on. Years in which I truly lost myself.

༈

Fast forward to 1981, the year I got sober and things began to change. It's funny, if you are an alcoholic and you put down booze, things start to get better right away. Like a crocus, peeking its head up from under the snow, I slowly emerged into this landscape of my new life. Getting honest with myself—putting down the drink—allowed me to take a hard look at all the ways I wasn't taking care of myself, with food, money, and sex. Little by little, changes started to occur.

I'd like to tell you that at five years of sobriety, I was fixed. But that is not my story. At five years, my eyes were just starting to see. There is a poem I love, by Emily Dickinson. A stranger recited it to me on a bus one day, in 1976, when I was traveling from my college into Boston. I didn't understand it then, but it makes perfect sense to me now:

> We play at Paste –
> Till qualified, for Pearl –
> Then, drop the Paste –
> And deem Ourself a fool –

> The shapes – tho' – were similar –
> And our new Hands
> Learned *Gem*-Tactics –
> Practicing *Sands* –[16]

What this poem says to me about self-love is that we have to learn it, earn it, through repeated practice. Life is a process of turning the fake into the real, moving from scales to concertos, from sketches to the Mona Lisa. Learning to love ourselves is like that. It takes work, patience, and persistence.

༈

For the first thirty years of my recovery, I played with the "paste" of self-love. I did good things for myself and other people, but it was all shadow compassion. For example, I took over a food train for a couple whose young son was dying of a complicated disease, and I organized meals for almost a year. I visited people who were sick, sent them cards, and brought them flowers. I offered to give young mothers relief from their babies. These were all good things, and there were many more. An outsider might look at this and say, "How kind!" But really, I was doing this because I felt a sense of "should," not "want to." I was simply mastering "sweet." I didn't really know how to love others, only how to act *as if* I loved others. Because I really did *not* love myself.

෴

In 2012, I was let go from my job teaching English at our local high school in Mooresville, North Carolina. As much as I both loved and loathed that position, it had provided me with the armor I needed to protect myself from feeling worthless on this planet. I knew it was not the right job for me—I stressed about it every day, trying to make engaging lesson plans and to relate to my students—but every day I felt myself sinking deeper and deeper into the quicksand. The firing came as something of a relief.

For a moment.

And then I was panicked. All I saw myself as was an alcoholic with bipolar disorder who couldn't hold a job. I was pinched by the limitations of my diseases, felt that I could not escape and ever be free of their hold. Although I had not had a drink for more than thirty years, and I had certainly improved my life, I still lacked the joy of living that was so often spoken of by my friends. I wondered why it had eluded me. I felt worthless to my family, to the world. I contemplated ending my life. Then my husband got sick, and suddenly I found myself in a new role as caretaker. I watched him degenerate from liver cancer, turning various shades of gray and yellow and losing his capacity to think, until that fatal day when the surgeon at Mayo Clinic told him there was no hope. He gave Thom three months to live. That was in 2015. Soon after, Thom survived a liver transplant, truly by the grace of God, and now works as, among other things, a certified personal trainer at the YMCA.

When I was faced with the very real possibility of my husband's death, suddenly, all the goodness in me rallied together, bubbled up, and set a new intention for life. Morbid musings over suicide seemed so self-indulgent and just plain wrong in light of my husband's circumstances. I knew—just as I had known in the dream of the henchman from so many years before—that I wanted not just to survive but to *live*. I made that intention clear to the Universe.

Since then, life has been nothing short of miraculous. I have learned how to discern honest sweetness from pretend sweetness. I have gotten off my own back. I no longer punish myself with harsh words or judgement. I look at myself with the eyes of a loving parent, correcting myself gently when necessary, and guiding myself to better choices. I listen to my inner voice in even the smallest things, asking what will bring joy. I don't presume to know the answer. I wait to be surprised.

Let me give you an example: Our old, black tea kettle started to leak, so we needed a new one. Now, Thom and I are older, living on a fixed income. We don't have a lot of extra money lying around to buy tea kettles and such. Still, I set off to Target with the intention of returning with a bright red, whistling tea kettle. When I got to the store, I looked at all the kettles and they were more than I could afford. Suddenly, I noticed a box marked "Clearance" on the lowest shelf. I picked it up. Inside was a cheery, yellow, whistling kettle in pristine condition—and for dirt cheap. Just what I was looking for! I took it home, and there it sits, bright as a daffodil on our black stove, whistling away. I tell you this story because one of the ways I have learned to love myself is to allow joy in. Letting myself be surprised by all the gifts the Universe offers me sends me into peals of laughter.

TOOLKIT #7

KEEP A JOURNAL. My entire recovery program is rooted in my relationship with a Greater Power. Divine Love. God. Universal Order. Call it what you will, every day, without fail, I turn my life and will over to that Power, to Its care. And it works.

Part of my self-care practice is journaling. I began writing my 'Morning Pages'—thank you again, Julia Cameron, author of *The Artist's Way*—in 1998. I can't imagine beginning a day without them. My pages are the spiritual Zamboni that clears the ice rink of my day. They let me start a new twenty-four hours with a clean slate and open the channel that allows my Higher Power to enter into my life. They have allowed me to love the person who I am, not who I think I should be.

TAKE YOUR MEDICATION: As a person with bipolar disorder, I must take my medication as prescribed, *even when I don't think I need it anymore.* And I must be honest with my doctor if I feel I am starting to slip into the highs or slide into the lows. I can't tell you how many people I know who have gone off their medication and suffered because of it. *Died* because of it. I love myself, so I take my meds as prescribed.

Note: if you are on medication and it's not working for you, don't just go off "cold turkey." Speak to your doctor. If your doctor isn't working for you, find another doctor. I have been through both these scenarios and what saved me was my tenacity. I refused to give up on myself. Please, don't give up on yourself. There is a solution to your situation.

AGAIN, MAKE YOUR BED. I was never in the military (although I did attend a British girls' boarding school—same thing) but I appreciate the ritual of making my bed. Every day, I smooth the sheets, pull the covers up, and tuck in the bedspread. I give permission for my day to begin in an orderly fashion. At the very least, it is one right thing I have done for myself that I can put on the plus side of my inventory at night. Making my bed lets my Higher Power know I am serious about doing this day right. What happens after that is up to God!

SHOWER AND BRUSH YOUR TEETH. This goes without saying, right? Not necessarily. When I am not practicing self-love, I let my hair get greasy, my teeth get fuzzy, and my armpits stink. I know when I use my daily cleanser and moisturizer and make sure to shave my legs, I am really treating my body like the temple it is.

Self-care is all about being mindful and slowing down enough to value who we are. For me, the three-stage dental care my daughter has prescribed—brushing with an electric toothbrush, and using a water flosser and whitening strips—is often more than I want to do. But I try to do it anyway, knowing how good my teeth will feel when I am done. If I want to have a nice smile, this is what needs to be done. The same is true of so many other facets of self-care. I need to be mindful, not lazy, if I want results in my life.

EAT HEALTHY. My usual breakfast is two eggs and a piece of fruit. I make sure I eat breakfast every day. For years I went without it, telling myself that once I started eating, I would never stop. I don't listen to that nonsense anymore. Today, I eat three healthy meals, with maybe a snack of fruit or nuts sometime in the afternoon. I allow myself to eat each day in a way that fuels my body rather than starving or stretching it. I am not organic or gluten-free. I don't do Keto or Paleo or Atkins. I just eat food that is nourishing and healthy. And every once in a while, I'll have a piece of wedding or birthday cake, or some Valentine's chocolate. No harm, no foul. I don't use a special occasion as an excuse to binge.

DRINK WATER. When I get up in the morning, before I even have my first cup of coffee, I drink two big glasses of water. I love the way it feels, the flavorless cold running through my veins like a mountain stream. It continues the process I began with my journaling, smoothing out my being, making way for the Divine to enter in. I keep this going throughout the day. It is so important to stay hydrated. Even when I am in the pool, swimming length after length, I need my water bottle to keep me from getting dizzy and passing out. I only have to think of my plants, how shriveled and limp they become if I forget to water them, to appreciate just how important water is to me.

I also had an eye-opening reminder of how critical it is for me to stay hydrated when my doctor told me I was experiencing chronic kidney disease.* This stemmed from the fact that I have been on lithium for so long. Part of the antidote, he told me, was to drink water, and plenty of it. So, now I make an effort to drink at least eight eight-ounce glasses of water a day.

WEAR CLOTHING YOU LOVE. As one who grew up wearing school uniforms all her life, I never was much of a slave to fashion. That, and my size, could have something to do with it. One week I was a size six, the next a sixteen. What wardrobe could keep up with that? When my kids were little, I spent a fortune buying them clothes from Hanna Andersson and OshKosh B'gosh, while I, a stay-at-home mom, shopped at Goodwill for pants with stretchy waists and oversized tops. Thank God those days are gone!

* See Author's Note at the end of the book.

I'll never turn down a nice hand-me-down, but if you give me clothes that don't seem like me, I will pass them right along.

Today, I only wear clothes that make me happy. The Irish cardigan my daughter brought back from her travels is well broken in. The brown UGG boots that Thom gave me for Christmas some years back are stained. The black V-neck cashmere sweater I bought for myself is one of my favorites. The point is, I don't ever leave the house looking like someone else. It has taken me a long time to know what I want to look like, and I want to look like me.

EXERCISE. My husband is a certified personal trainer. He works out at the gym for at least two hours a day. I tried the weight routines, circuits, treadmills, and ellipticals. That is not where I find my joy. Once, long ago, I found my joy in running, but those days are gone. Today, I get my exercise in the water where I participate in water aerobics with twenty-five or more other seniors, or swimming laps—a mile (or seventy pool lengths) three times per week. I supplement that exercise with yoga and walking, two to three miles down to the park and back. My exercise program may not be featured in *Women's Health* magazine, but it is the one I enjoy and stick with. What good would it do to have a gym routine if I never went? A big part of self-love is loving yourself. Not caring what other people are doing or saying about what you should do.

TAKE PAUSE. Sometimes my life is so rich and full that I get going and I forget to stop. Then I will notice our spotted cat in the window, licking her paws and lying down to gaze outside. Of course! *Paws!*

Stopping, pausing in a day, is a necessary ingredient in self-love. For one, it reminds me that I am simply not that important. The world will whirl without my spinning it. I have to remember, as someone once told me, that I am a human being, not a human doing. When I get quiet and breathe, my inner spirit nudges me toward a cup of tea and a good book, or maybe a phone call to a friend who needs encouragement, or a gentle walk to see how the seasons are progressing. Always, I need to remember to breathe and to let my life breathe, not to corset it tightly in too much activity. It is often in these quiet moments that I feel most at peace with myself.

SLEEP. Who can survive without it? I have been told that nobody ever died from lack of sleep, but I don't believe it. I know when I am sleep deprived, my judgement muddies and my thinking goes south. I need sleep. I strive to get eight hours a night. Since I am up at four o'clock most mornings, that means I am in bed by eight o'clock at night "Grandma hours." Or, as I like to think of them, Ben Franklin hours. Wasn't it he who said, "Early to bed and early to rise, makes a man healthy, wealthy, and wise"? Proper sleep keeps me balanced and balance, is what I aim for in my recovery. If I have skimped on the eight hours at night, I will make it up with a delicious nap sometime in the afternoon. Anywhere from fifteen minutes to an hour, I will indulge in rest. I am a happier person for it!

DARE TO CHANGE. Before I had my spiritual experience in 2015 and decided to really start *living* my life, I lived in fear and in worry about so many things. Intellectually, I knew it was silly to brood over traffic and weather and people—all things I could not change—but I did it anyway.

A number of years ago, I accompanied my oldest sister down to her house in Florida. We drove to her home in The Villages, a community for fifty-five and over; I was to fly back. When the time came to leave, I was frantic, convinced the plane would crash and I would never see my husband and children again. I broke down in the airport, sobbing uncontrollably, so riddled with fear I almost could not walk. Of course, the plane did not crash, as I am here to tell the story.

There were so many other areas in my life in which I was afraid. When Thom almost died, we had a day of quiet reflection. I cannot speak for him, but I reached deep into my soul with all this acute fear and dread, and asked for God's help. This is what I heard: "Everything is going to be alright. Everything is alright." That message changed my life. Everything is alright. No matter what is going on around me, if I am close to the Divine Will, everything is alright.

Because of that assurance, I have been able to do things that before seemed impossible—everything from merging onto I-77 at rush hour or zip lining at the U.S. National Whitewater Center to writing and publishing my books and poems. Oh, and teaching again. And flying on planes without melting down. There is nothing I cannot do if I am connected to Universal Power.

The fun thing about beginning to dare is that it is addictive, in a good way. Once I started to try new things, like tubing on the New River and making meals I'd never cooked before, I gained confidence in myself. I allowed myself to begin to play with my life and, thus, to enjoy it more. The more I play, the happier I am. The happier I am, the more useful I can be to others. Isn't that what self-love is all about: getting to the point where we can be of maximum service to ourselves and others?

To *feel* joy is to *share* joy. Self-love is the beginning to a joy-filled life. Don't believe me? Implement these suggestions for ninety days. If your life hasn't changed dramatically for the better, contact me. I will gladly refund your misery!

CHAPTER 8
The Guest Room

*I*n remodeling a house, one of the most important features, in my mind, is the guest room. Perhaps it is the influence of all those years studying classic Greek literature in college that led me to this. In ancient times, people believed the gods disguised themselves as strangers, so the Greeks always kept a bed prepared and an extra place set at the table in case one should casually pop in, (not good to piss off the gods, especially Zeus and Athena, who made it a habit of showing up unexpectedly).

In most of the places I have lived as an adult, we haven't had the space to set aside for visitors. Nevertheless, accommodations have been made, throwing sleeping bags on the couch or inflating—wonder of wonders— the queen-sized air mattress. Who knew that something made of plastic and air could be so comfortable?

There was the time when my daughter brought home a dozen or more of her Habitat for Humanity friends as they passed through on their way to a site. The students, darling and flexible as they were, found any space they could on the hardwood floors of our little ranch home, grateful for running water and the roof over their heads.

The point is, making space for strangers is an important practice, both in remodeling a home and in reconstructing a life.

Recently, I had lunch with a friend who was going through an unpleasant divorce. He spoke with me of his loneliness, and his desire to meet new people, both male and female, something he had not made an effort to do in his twenty-five years of marriage. He had been glued to his wife. I listened to his words, so filled with hunger for connection, then cautioned him to be careful about just who he invited into his life.

When I was using drugs and alcohol, I put all the wrong people on my guest list. My guest room was filled with people who were abusive and cruel. I brought that on myself, though I do attribute many of my bad choices to bipolar disorder and alcoholism. For example, when I was nineteen and involuntarily sentenced to take a semester off from college due to my erratic behavior, I worked at our local Howard Johnson's restaurant, dishing out coffee and Indian pudding. One day, a man came in who looked to me exactly like Robert Redford. He sat at the counter, drinking coffee and flirting, casually, as customers often did. My mind convinced me that this was the famous actor, the Sundance

Kid, making me blush. Of course, he was not Robert Redford. He was an adulterous businessman from New Jersey with no good on his mind. He treated me very badly, and I let him. I opened my guest room to him.

Today, I no longer regret the abuse and shame that went along with being with that man. If anything, those weeks reveal to me just how sick and damaged I was. Whenever I think of going off my medication—which, now, is never—I only have to think of him and the band of brothers he brought along with him in his car one night, and I am instantly reminded of how I never again want to ask him or anyone like him into my life again. Though I have never been certain if what he and his half dozen friends did to me in the state park that winter evening qualified as gang rape, I know that I went with them only because I felt I had no other option. I was trapped and they would not take "no" for an answer.

Rape is a terrible, complicated, and frequently misunderstood event. When I was previously married to a Boston lawyer, I accompanied him on occasion to rape trials, under the auspices of gathering information for a book. Secretly, I wanted to hear those women's stories, to connect with women who had gone through what I had been through, not just once but three times. I was devastated when I saw how the courts leaned, the other lawyers insisting the women "asked for it" or "got what they deserved." I was reminded of Zeus (him again) in the old myths, and how he forced himself on the naked Daphne, who was bathing herself in a crystal pool, as though he'd had a right to take her sexually just because he was a god. *The* god.

I have met men like that. Men who insisted that my pretty looks and youth gave them the right to hold me down, threaten me with a crystal ashtray over my head, and force themselves on me as I babysat my two nephews who were sleeping upstairs. I was living with my oldest sister in Connecticut at the time. I was so unhinged by the rape. I had had plenty of sex before, but never like that. I believe it threw me into a mental state I had never known. My solution was to run away. I met a couple at work, another Howard Johnson's, from Oregon who needed someone to drive them back across the country. The husband had had an onset of eczema and could not handle the trip. So, I volunteered, went back to my sister's that night and told her I was leaving. The next day I was gone.

They were a pleasant enough couple. We took the scenic route, stopping at Niagara Falls for a helicopter ride and visiting the Corn Palace, but there were nights, too, when after they had retired, I hit the hotel bar and ended up in some stranger's bed. As always, when I drank, I never knew where it would take me. When we arrived in Oregon, I learned that I could not work as a bartender for them as I was only nineteen, so I ran away to a friend's place in LA.

I had known this friend from college. He was sweet on me, but I was repelled by him. I just needed someone, and somewhere to stay. The weeks spent with him were a disaster. I searched relentlessly for a job but found none. All the while, my drinking and my delusions were accelerating. I see now that at that time, I was manic in full.

When I was finally given a chance to work as a waitress at a diner in LA, I imagined that one of the customers was Sal Mineo and he wanted to rescue me. I don't recall the specifics, but the diner let me go. The only other offer I had was as a prostitute, "working undercover" the guy on the corner had told me as he tried to persuade me to go with him. I wonder how many young girls are now in the same situation that I was in then.

One day I stood outside Schwab's Pharmacy in my sleeveless blue shirt dress, looking like a wholesome farm girl from Vermont, convinced I would be discovered like Lana Turner. All that happened was that I was picked up by a phony movie producer who told me he was Tony Curtis's brother. He took me to a graveyard and forced me to give him a blow job there, then dropped me off with my friend who, frustrated by my antics, beat me up. We decided, mutually, that it was time for me to go home.

I will never know what my parents were really feeling at the time. Angry. Disappointed. Worried. I only know that I was kept home for the semester and worked back at the old Howard Johnson's in our hometown, and the cycles of mania and depression continued, unidentified. A parade of strangers entering my life. Unwanted guests. It shouldn't be a crime to be pretty. Or young. Or female. It shouldn't be a crime to have a mental illness that makes you lose your judgement and tells you things that are not real. Thankfully, not all men are predators. But some are.

જ

It bears repeating that when my father died in 1997, a giant hole ripped through my soul. And not mine only. All my sisters were deeply affected by his death. However, my grief for the father who had meant so much to me opened the door to mania in a way that I had never experienced before. Bear in mind that this all happened before I even knew I had bipolar disorder; I had not yet been diagnosed.

As I have said, I began to meet regularly with my parish priest, a very ethical and compassionate man. Call it Freudian or psychological transference, but I became deeply attached to Father "X." My feelings expanded, and I tried, repeatedly, to encourage him into a relationship with me, because sex seemed like the only remedy for the pain I felt. I know now my feelings for him were not real. I wasn't in love with him, never was. And I am so grateful he was a skilled practitioner who knew my grief for what it was and didn't take advantage of me.

Not so with the asshole chaplain at the seminary where I worked, whom I went to see when Father 'X' was on vacation. My mania was so acute at this time that I saw this man as a god, which went straight to his ego. In truth, he was an aging, ugly, self-centered predator who took my disorder and ran with it. Our brief affair almost blew up my current marriage and definitely shaped the rest of my life.

⌣

This is painful stuff to write about, but I share it because it is important for me to own just how faulty my choice in guests can be. Even when I am not in the throes of mania, I invite people into my life who are not healthy for me—naysayers who don't support my dreams, critics who quash my enthusiasm, negative thinkers who drag me down. There are those, too, who seem to be on my side, and who are well-meaning enough, but who lack courtesy and whose concept of a relationship is very one-sided: *I'll use you; you stroke my ego.*

The thought occurs to me, are these people really negative influences in my life, or is it the filter through which I see them? Often, I find that a person who rubs me the wrong way one day is miraculously changed the next time we meet, after I have had a good night's sleep, a hot meal, and a spot of meditation. Was it them, or was I the one at fault?

The longer I live, the clearer it becomes that my prejudices against people are just that: *my* prejudices. But if I practice self-love, I am much more inclined to feel compassion toward those around me. I am not going to like everybody, nor am I going to go on a canoe trip with them, as my first husband used to say, but I can show love for everyone. Especially myself.

Saying that, I realize there are times when I need to have my thoughts monitored and my enthusiasm brought down a notch. Then I have to be certain I am turning to trustworthy sources for guidance. When, for example, my husband notes I seem a little "off," I need to listen to him rather than assume I know what is best.

This practice did not come easily to one who was as stubborn, willful, and controlling as I used to be. Let someone else tell me what to do? Never! ... Until those *nevers* began to accumulate into a pile of apologies for my misguided actions, and I recognized I needed help. Today, I listen to others—even when I don't want to, or when their suggestions are as tight as a rubber band around my head—because I may glean something that is just what I need to hear at that moment.

～

So, how do I go about putting people on my guest list and inviting them into my life? Well, I am not sure *I* put them on the list at all. It has been my experience that people are placed in my path and then, and only then, do I decide whether to learn what it is they have to teach me.

There is a big difference between a true friend who stays on that list forever and a one-night stand who flashes through. Back to my recently divorced friend. He is lonely, so he has gone on a date or two. He asked me, as I licked my ice cream cone in the ice cream parlor where he worked, "How do I know whether I really want this person in my life?" He admitted he has a tendency to go all or nothing into a relationship, and for years he lived in a state of codependency with his former spouse. So my question to him was, "Have you changed or are you still the codependent who takes people hostage when you meet them?" A true friend lets go, leaves breathing room, and isn't threatened by departure. The codependent leaves claw marks down the calves of the one who has the gall to walk away. The next thing I knew, he had moved from North Carolina back to New Jersey. That's one way of dealing with a difficult relationship, I guess, though I am fairly sure it is not a long-term solution.

After our blow up in 1998 that resulted from my affair, my husband and I recognized our own codependency. We went, individually, to a codependency treatment center in Pennsylvania called Chit Chat.[17] At Chit Chat, I learned how to put the focus on myself in a healthy way, how to engage in self-care, and how to stop blaming or burdening my husband with my insecurities. One of the most valuable tools I took away from the center was the technique of speaking from the "I" position. For example, instead of saying, "You really piss me off when you leave the water dripping in the shower," rephrase the issue and own your feelings. Say instead, "I am bothered by the water dripping in the shower." Probably a poor example, but the only one I could think of as I hear the water going *plink plink* as I write. The solution is for me to get up and turn the water off myself.

Which brings me to another example. I like to have the dishes done in the evening before we go to bed. I also like to have my husband do them, because I have, generally, prepared the meal. However, there was a time when he left the dishes soaking in the sink so that he could relax at night and do them in the morning. This became an issue between us, so important that we took it to therapy. When I told my side of the story, my therapist looked at me and said, "What do you want? If you want Thom to do the dishes, let them wait until morning. If you want them done at night, do them yourself." The solution is often just that simple. I have to stop basing my emotions on what others do—or do not—do.

Until then, I had no idea that most of my words were based on *you*—what you thought, what you felt—as if I had any idea. At Chit Chat, I came face to face with the truth that I did not really know my husband. I only knew my image of who he *should* be. In essence, I had spent years in a relationship with myself.

That was twenty years ago. Since then, our marriage has been through many trials, but today we have a healthy, differentiated relationship in which we live side by side, supporting one another, rather than choking the life out of each other like pernicious vines. We each pursue our own goals and dreams, while coming together often to connect with each other and reaffirm our love.

∽

My "guest room" is like a bed and breakfast; people come and go. Some regulars return. Some I never see again, but always there is flow. The most challenging relationships are those with my family of origin. There is a part of me, leftover from my childhood, that believes I will not be complete until all six of us sisters are huddled in the guest room bed like the ten little monkeys jumping on the bed. But you know what happened to the monkeys, right? One by one they toppled to the floor until there was just one little monkey left.

Why the insistence on my part that we all get along? My sisters and I were born into the same family, that is true, but each of us has chosen a unique path. And maybe we don't really like each other at all, though we may love each other dearly. When I try to push any of my sisters into a relationship with me, I suffer, because they are simply being who they are and haven't chosen me as a friend. It hurts. But *they* aren't hurting me; I am hurting me.

And that brings me to the most important guest of all: God. Every morning, I turn my life and my will over to my Higher Power's care. I don't know how it works. But I do know that when I invite the Divine into my life on a regular basis, with consistency and conviction, all the other relationships in my life go much more smoothly. I am able, with God's help, to view others and myself with compassion. The petty differences and hurts from long ago melt away. I am able to embrace our differences, even celebrate them.

Is this to say that everything is made perfect? No. I still despise the men who raped me. I still question the ethics of the man with whom I had an affair. I still cringe a little when I hear that *tone* in one of my sisters' voices. But with Divine help, I forgive myself for these reactions and carry on, eager to meet the next teacher on my path.

The guest room is a place where I can sit, ponder, and reflect, where I can hear my inner yearnings, where the Universe will respond, and where new souls will enter in.

It is my spiritual salon, for it is only in our connections with others that we discover who we truly are.

In the guest room, I have no expectations. I allow people to flow into my life and to change me. These are the people who are meant to be there. From the chance encounter with a secretary at church to deeper engagements with my children, if I am attentive to the energy and cues I receive from others, I can make a decision as to whether or not a relationship is healthy for me. If this sounds like a contradiction—like I am taking over God's job—it is not. As a human being, I always have the right to exercise my free will. And one way to do that is to learn to say no. I will not allow people who do not have my best interests at heart into my world, no matter what their relationship to me. I don't need to put up walls or make rules about allowing people into my life. But I do need to enter into all encounters with eyes wide and heart open, trusting that the true powers of the world will allow me to discern just who I should invite in.

TOOLKIT #8

Sometimes the people I invite into my guest room are invited intentionally. Sometimes they are invited accidentally, seemingly introduced to me by the Universe that thinks I have something to learn. Whatever the case, here are some tools I use when discerning who I am going to allow into my sacred space.

KNOW YOUR MOTIVATION. For me, personally, this is one of the most important factors in letting people in. If I am honest about my motivation, then I can begin a relationship on solid ground. When, for example, I ask a friend who is in school for digital marketing to help me with my website, I need to be clear. This is not about being friends; it is not about having lunch at his house. It is about a business proposition, nothing more.

I didn't always used to function that way. If I wanted something from you—your expertise, your attention, your support—I would come at things sideways, making promises I could not keep and putting on a false persona of friendship. Don't get me wrong. There is nothing bad about being friendly, but when I manipulate my emotions and yours to get what I want, that is wrong. It is important to call a spade a spade. If I need your help or support, I ask for it. If you turn me down, so be it. But then there is none of that gray area of pretense that can ooze into the situation, causing all sorts of potential harm.

So, before you ask a person into your life, ask yourself this: Why am I inviting him or her in? Be honest. Be clear. Save everyone some heartache.

SET REASONABLE BOUNDARIES. A fence works both ways. It keeps intruders out, but it also contains me inside my space. Two of the culprits that plagued me the most in relationships well into my sobriety were codependency and people pleasing. As a codependent, I relied on *you* to tell *me* how I felt about myself, my life. I had no voice of my own. I was wrapped around you like a thread on a spool, choking the breath out of any interaction we had. The catch was that I was not in a relationship with you; I held you hostage.

When I had my manic meltdown in 1998, my husband and I, both codependents, didn't know how to deal with one another. We loved each other deeply but were so entwined, the hurt we inflicted on each other seemed too great to heal. That is when we went to Chit Chat codependency retreat center and learned how to live and let live. There, each at our own separate times, we began to grasp the idea that we must love ourselves first if we are to ever love anyone else. "Me First" but not "Me Only." It was a painful process, undoing all those bad, selfish behaviors. Thank heavens it was gradual, we stuck it out, and we are now in a place in our lives where we are codependent no more (thank you, Melody Beattie); we love ourselves *and* each other.

A second culprit in unhealthy relationships is people pleasing, which actually ties into codependency. People pleasers don't have any sense of who they really are. They depend entirely upon other people's reactions to them to dictate what they do and say. From the outside, people pleasers seem genuine enough and very obliging. They are the ones always giving compliments, congenial to a fault, excessively kind. There is nothing wrong with saying nice things, doing nice things, being nice, but when those characteristics are taken to the extreme, when they interfere with other people's lives, that is a problem. A difficulty people pleasers have is that they don't know what to do in the absence of others. They don't know who they are, where they stop and others begin. They are almost frantic in their efforts to make others happy. Meanwhile, inside, they are miserable and lost. People pleasers can't have relationships with others because they don't have a relationship with themselves. The antidote to this, of course, is self-care.

BE OPEN TO NEW TEACHERS. Most of the people living in my guest room are ones I never sought intentionally but who God placed on my horizon. These are the friends and acquaintances I have made as a result of showing up to life and seeing who comes along (not that I was looking).

I think specifically of one woman, a good friend now, who I met one day in a water-jogging class. I rarely go water jogging, but I did on that day. I saw a lovely woman enter the pool, and as we jogged, side by side, we struck up a conversation. She is an artist and was having a tough time writing an application for a residency. I, the writer, gave her some suggestions. Class ended. We parted ways. Later, I saw her again. She had taken my suggestions and incorporated them into her statement and actually won the residency! She and I have been friends since, sharing lunch, congratulating one another on our successes (though hers are far more significant than mine). The point is, the Universe brought us together at that moment, and we were there for each other.

I can't begin to tell you how many other instances like that there have been in my life. Actually, just about everyone I meet I see as a teacher who has something to show me about myself that will help me grow. From the produce clerk at our local grocery store to the postmistress, the booksellers at the bookstore to the assistant pastor at the local church, there is something to be taken from all interactions— and given too. Relationships are not one-sided. I have to remember I have something to offer to those I communicate with.

In short, be open to all possibilities, even to those people who seem offensive or rub you the wrong way. They are often the ones we learn the most from, especially as we watch our feelings change in regard to them. Which brings me to my last tool ....

PRACTICE COMPASSION. Great spiritual leaders like the Dalai Lama, Archbishop Tutu, Pema Chödrön, and Jimmy Carter have taught me a lot about practicing compassion. But the teaching is not enough. Compassion has to move from the head to the heart if the world is ever to heal from its wounds. Are you just singing, "Love, love, love", or are you actually loving your fellows?

Loving and practicing compassion are actually two different things. I practice compassion when I allow people to be who they are, exactly who they are, without insisting they be more like me or fit into some mold I have created. I don't have to like them, but I can pray that the suffering they feel will be relieved. It would be presumptuous of me to assume that I know what is best for everyone, for this world. I can only know myself, and sometimes that is plenty hard enough. Having compassion for myself when I make a mistake or do something mean is sometimes difficult. But if I cannot have compassion for myself, how can I have it for anyone else?

The difficulty I find is that my brain leaps naturally into passing judgement, criticizing, and finding fault with others. There is some old tape in there that says to me, "You need to be better than everyone else." I sigh when I hear that voice, take it up in my arms and soothe it. "There, there, Hopie. You are feeling insecure again. I feel your suffering. May it be removed." If I can soothe my own suffering, be gentle with myself, I can be gentle with others. It doesn't excuse their bad ways, but it removes me from thinking I can do anything about it. I'll pray for them and leave the results to God.

CHAPTER 9
Establishing Curb Appeal

One of the last steps that is taken when remodeling a house is establishing curb appeal. Even if you are not intending to sell your fixer upper, you still want to make sure the outsides of the house reflect the care and attention you have given the inside. Think about it. If you are looking for a home to buy, what is the first thing you see? The exterior. If the house is nicely painted, the lawn tended to, and the shrubs out front trimmed and cared for, someone is more likely to want to visit than if there are old bicycles on the front lawn and rubbish strewn about. Even if it *is* tidy, if the paint is cracked and peeling and the shutters list to the left, potential buyers may pass this place by (unless they want to take it on as a project and fix it themselves).

The same is true of a person. How I look affects how people respond to me. I am not suggesting I need to wear designer jeans and carry an expensive handbag, or even that such a uniform is appealing. But my curb appeal has to do with how I present myself to the world. Do I want to come across as sloppy, unkempt, and undesirable? Do I greet each morning with a scowl, surly and unapproachable? Or do I want to clean up, show up, and put my best foot forward? And I really mean *my* best foot forward. The thing is, my best foot and your best foot will undoubtedly be different. But if I can be the best me I can be, that is all the Universe asks of me.

ﻼ

With humans, curb appeal, composed of the superficial things we own or wear, has become the measure by which we see ourselves and present our *persona* to the world. Buying expensive cars, clothes, and country homes has become the way in which we set our "value." If we have less than an Audi or a Range Rover, less than a 3,500-square-foot home (on the lake), less than season tickets to the Panthers games or the Charlotte Symphony, less than month-long trips overseas to the far East, Egypt, or Europe, we feel just that—less than. And often we judge other people by the amount of stuff they have too, be it a lot or a little.

Being wealthy and having nice things is not inherently bad. It's not a criminal act (in most cases) to be rich. However, our society's fascination with money has led us to marginalize those who can't afford whitening strips for the perfect smile, those who may not have any dental or medical coverage at all.

As a society, we value celebrity and wealth. Drawn to the rich and famous like bees to a honeypot, many of us spend our lives and the little income we have chasing the American dream. We play the lottery earnestly believing we will morph into one of the rich and famous overnight. I know I have been seduced by magazines that offer a very one-sided image of what success and happiness look like. In their pages, I see images of flawless men and women diving into crystal blue waters, their near-naked bodies tanned to perfection, not a hair out of place, not a wrinkle or an ounce of fat. Perfection. Perfect curb appeal.

I'm not buying that lie anymore. I used to buy it. I used to drive my Volvo while wearing my designer shoes and carrying my Coach bag, tan from a trip to the islands, flush and conceited and self-satisfied. I guess I attracted people when I was thin and golden, dancing in my tiny designer jeans with my white linen blouse, ending up in a relationship outside my first marriage. I still see myself, bathing suit painted to my body, smiling at the camera for my lover while my ex-husband toiled away as a lawyer. I may have had curb appeal, but I had no morals, heart, or soul. What made me drink the lemonade of self-preoccupation and materialism? I think it was my insecurity, my dependency on other people to tell me I was okay.

༄

I've talked about my Boston lawyer ex-husband; he was a charismatic Irishman with a big singing voice. But he was also an active alcoholic, twenty-five years my senior, who could never really be there for me. That's no excuse for my behavior, I realize. Still, our marriage ended not because of my extra-marital affairs but because I got pregnant.

When I got pregnant, he didn't want me to have the baby. He already had three grown children, and he didn't want another one. Honestly, I think, he didn't want me to be a mother; he wanted me to be his plaything—the artsy girl who ran marathons and published poems. I was not strong enough at that time to stick up for myself. I honestly didn't even know who "myself" was. The even greater truth was that I didn't want to give up drinking for nine months, nor did I think I could.

As soon as I left the abortion clinic in 1979, I knew I had done a terrible thing for my soul. I had not been true to myself. I had taken a life that was not mine to take. I blamed my ex-husband as I was not able at the time to take personal responsibility. Our marriage was over then, though we didn't divorce for another two years. As time has passed over the decades, I have come to recognize that decision as one of the lowest moments of my active alcoholism. I pray for that baby—that little girl—often, apologizing for taking her life but thanking her for the push that led to my sobriety. (I am not saying that abortion is wrong or that it is not wrong. I am saying that abortion was wrong for me. In all instances like this, a woman must get very quiet with herself and ask what her truth is. What choice will she be able to live with for the rest of her life?)

꒜

Focusing on curb appeal doesn't always have to lead us down such dark alleys. Sometimes a preoccupation with nice things is simply the reward of having worked hard and well. Take the family that lives in a beautiful home on the water, buys expensive wine, and travels all over the world. These may be people who have worked hard and enjoy beautiful things. Certainly, they are entitled to their lifestyle. Perhaps they give back to their communities. Their curb appeal is genuine because they are genuinely loving and generous.

This is not so with the woman who goes under the knife so much that she is barely recognizable. Here is a woman who wants to look a certain way, who hopes to mimic the smooth skin and ageless beauty of a movie star, but who ends up a monster. Her curb appeal, based on a superficial goal, often has a negative effect.

Traditional curb appeal, fundamentally, works from the outside in. What you see on the outside is supposedly what you will get on the inside. If I get my hair cut and colored, have a mani-pedi, and wear an expensive suit and shoes, you may think—when I step out of my Cadillac—that I am successful. That I have arrived.

But have I really? What is going on *inside*? What am I thinking? Feeling? What isn't that plastic smile, plastered across my face, telling you? That my home has been destroyed in a near-fatal fire? That our child died of an overdose? That our house is being foreclosed on? While none of these things has actually happened to me, they have happened to people I care about. And the only reason I know about these tragedies is because they were shared. People will never know who I am, how I am, as long as I keep it all together, maintain my composure as if I'm doing "all right." This all amounts to: "I am shutting you out and going it alone."

Worst idea ever.

Throughout my sobriety, I have practiced "telling on myself." I keep no secrets from my husband, my sponsor, or the group. Secrets will keep you sick and lead you back to a drink. So, I embarrass myself repeatedly by confessing to all the dumb shit that goes on in my head. Just so I don't beat up on myself, I look at this action as my way of being a "Clown for God." When I am a clown, I am laughing at myself and with others over the myriad of ridiculous ideas that float through my mind. This balances me. It keeps me small when I am getting too BIG. It offers me humility.

And being a clown is part of my curb appeal. People often turn to me because they know just who I am and what they are getting. They feel comfortable with me because I feel comfortable with myself. There are no skeletons in my closet that I am trying to avoid. What you see is what you get, which smooths the way to a happier life, free from fear and guilt.

My new, non-traditional understanding of curb appeal is that it flows from the *inside* out. If I lead with my heart and soul from a spiritual perspective, if I practice compassion, tolerance, patience, perseverance, and love, then excessive materialism has no place in my life.

I am reminded of a recent trip my husband and I took to Arizona to spend time with our oldest daughter and her husband. There were so many exquisitely magical moments as we traveled around the state, visiting one national park after another. But I will never forget the searing beauty of the desert in bloom, the hills turned gold by an abundance of golden Mexican poppies. Standing on the hill, surrounded by those flowers and others—blue, white, pink—watching my daughter photograph every bloom, the wind gentle and warm, the silence wrapped around me like a shawl. When I think of that day, I am reminded of Matthew 6:25-29.

Do not be anxious about your life, what you shall eat or what you shall drink, nor about your body, what you shall put on. Is not life more than food, and the body more than clothing? Look at the birds of the air: they neither sow nor reap nor gather into barns, and yet your heavenly Father feeds them. Are you not of more value than they? And which of you by being anxious can add one cubit to his span of life? And why are you anxious about clothes? Consider the lilies of the field, how they grow; they neither toil nor spin; yet I tell you, even Solomon in all his glory was not arrayed like one of them. (The New Oxford Annotated Bible)

کئ

My sharing of this passage isn't to say I don't appreciate nice things. I do. But I don't have to have things to make me who I am. My thoughts go back to that old saying: "Bloom where you are planted."

If I am grateful and appreciative for all I have been given in life, in me just as I am; if I am mindful of who and what I have in my world; if I can simplify, cutting down to the core of my existence, I will be far happier than I ever was accumulating stuff. William Wordsworth speaks to just this in his poem, "The World Is Too Much with Us":

> The world is too much with us; late and soon,
> Getting and spending, we lay waste our powers;
> Little we see in Nature that is ours ....[18]

This poem speaks to me of the ills that plague our society. Materialism. Selfishness. Pretense. It is not anyone's fault, really, and yet we are all culpable. These faults have caused an epidemic from which we all suffer.

But there is hope!

Every day, I set my intention to be true to myself so the person I send out into the world is an honest reflection of my authentic self. I choose what I clothe myself in carefully, not because I am a fashionista— far from it!—but so I feel the outside connects with my inner feelings. I listen to my body as I go through the day and eat healthy food that will nourish me, not clog me up with sugars and fats. I pay attention to the music I listen to, the shows (if any) I watch on TV. I read positive words and exercise gently. All these daily practices, and more, heal me. Over time, my broken soul has been refurbished by a kind Universe. No longer chasing after attention and affection, I stand secure in the Divine Love that enfolds me.

Curb appeal is all about "attraction not promotion." I no longer have to chase life down with a butterfly net. My job is simply to be who I am, standing in the desert, surrounded by flowers, letting the butterflies come to me.

TOOLKIT #9

BE AUTHENTIC. A big part of making ourselves appealing is the recognition that we aren't going to appeal to everyone. Once I accepted this fact, I was free to evolve into my authentic self, to be who I truly am. Life is full of curious paradoxes. On the one hand, "what other people think about us is none of our business." Or as Ruiz states in *The Four Agreements*, "Don't take anything personally."[19] On the other hand, "The paradox is," says the Dalai Lama in *The Book of Joy*, "although the drive behind excessive self-focus is to seek greater happiness for yourself, it ends up doing exactly the opposite."[20] The following tools are like needles and thread, bringing together those two ideas so that as we focus on making ourselves more appealing to others, we don't lose ourselves in the process.

STICK WITH THE WINNERS. The world is so full of fakes, people who consciously go out of their way to scam you, and others who are simply unaware of what the scammers are doing. Whatever the cause, there are plenty of people running around who aren't really what they say they are. It is, therefore, refreshing to meet someone whose inside matches their outside. I know those people when I meet them. They look me in the eye, speak with sincerity and openness. They are not trying to impress me; nothing is staged. They don't hide behind makeup, clothes, or grand words; they simply are who they are. Plain and simple. Their words come from their hearts, not their backsides. I may not always agree with them, I may not like what they say, but at least they are genuine. I am drawn to that.

I think others are drawn to my genuine nature, as well. While my message may not always be what was anticipated, I believe people appreciate the sincerity behind my words. Whenever I open my mouth at a meeting or in private conversations (which is always), I ask the Universe to guide my words, that what I say might be of use to others. So far, this practice has worked out. Putting my trust in my Higher Power to keep me honest and open, frees me to speak from my heart. Evidently, that is attractive.

BE TRUSTWORTHY. One of the other most attractive characteristics of humans, I find, is their trustworthiness. If I can count on you to be trustworthy, and if I, in turn, am someone you can trust, that goes a long way toward building a solid relationship.

Being trustworthy has great curb appeal. Be where you say you are going to be when you say you are going to be there. Don't "borrow" and not return. Don't steal your best friend's boyfriend. Don't keep secrets from those you love and who love you. There should be no skeletons in your closet. Keep your word. Honestly, I find this last one difficult, especially around money. I buy into the idea that "I want what I want when I want it," so I use the credit card when I know I shouldn't or fudge the accounts a little. Someday I will grow out of this ... I hope.

My husband hopes so too. (We are actually making great strides in this area thanks to Dave Ramsey's *Total Money Makeover*. I highly recommend it for anyone who has money issues.)

BE POLITE. Politeness goes a long way toward drawing people to you. Not *phony* politeness (and we all know what that looks like, right?) but genuine politeness and respect: thanking people for comments and wishes made on Facebook, sending cards in recognition of kindness or gifts, letting someone in line in traffic, asking the cashier at the grocery store how his day is going.

Politeness has a lot to do with humility. I acknowledge that I am not superior to anyone, that I am dependent upon the generosity of others—whether that is my husband bringing me a cup of coffee every morning or a friend keeping her promise to attend my book launch. My life is as good as it is because of others who help me out. So, it is only polite to say, "Thank you." Those two little words go a long way.

SMILE! Everybody loves a smile. I am not suggesting you walk around like the Cheshire Cat with some shit-eating grin on your face, but be aware of the shape of your mouth. Is it generally turned down or generally turned up? Somewhere I heard that there are thousands of muscles in our face and when we smile, we use more calories than when we relax into a scowl. If you need a reason to smile, there's a good one. For me, when I catch myself with my mouth in a frown, I just lift the corners of my lips, not into a grin but into a Mona Lisa smile. I feel gratitude surge up in me and my mood is lifted. Why not smile? Why not be grateful for this amazing day? Why not spread joy?

BE KIND. A popular T-shirt reads, "In a world where you can be anything, be kind." I like that. Of all the choices I make on any given day, the choice to be kind is the best one. How hard is it to make bacon and eggs for my son on his day off, even though it interrupts my morning schedule? How much effort does it take to call a friend who may be suffering? How time-consuming is it to water my plants and play fetch with the dogs on a beautiful sunny day?

I am not thinking about being kind when I am doing these things, but I am thinking about others. As the Dalai Lama says, "The more we care for the happiness of others, the greater our own sense of happiness."[21] When I help someone perfect a cover letter, I feel happy that I can be of service, that my talents as a writer are both sought after and put to good use. When I give my plants a new home by digging holes, mixing soil, patting them in their beds, and soaking them, I am happy to be a part of Creation. When I reach out in kindness to anyone, anything, I feel connected to the Universe. I am no longer stuck in the bell-jar of self-centeredness. Kindness frees me. It makes me attractive to others who are drawn to this way of life that I lead.

CHAPTER 10
Color My World

One of the easiest ways to change the whole feel of a house is to paint it. That drab dining room takes on a new personality when you color it a deep red. The lifeless, navy front door welcomes in new friends when you paint it a cheery yellow. The idea here is not to just add color but to add color you love. Neutrals. Primaries. Pastels. Painting is about connecting with your inner designer.

But painting isn't just about the paint in the can. To paint properly requires patience and hard work. A big part of the painting process, the thing that makes it successful or not, is the preparation. Cleaning, spackling, taping, priming—these activities are a time-consuming but essential part of coloring walls, windows, and doors. Only when you have taken care with these preliminary steps can you truly benefit from painting.

～

On my journey toward self-transformation, I have been tempted by new hues that bring me joy. I have considered taking shortcuts in my recovery. Among these were my tendencies to rush through a thorough personal inventory when I needed to take my time, and to attempt to take control of situations that were none of my business. I thought I knew the answers when, really, I wouldn't have known what to do with the questions if they'd been placed in front of me on a silver tray. In my third year of recovery, I leapt at the opportunity to go to divinity school. I thought I had it all figured out. I would get to know God better and ensure my sobriety. Nothing could have been further from the truth. I came out poorer, more confused, and less qualified for a career in teaching than when I went in. The only good thing about the experience was that I ended up in Princeton with a teaching contract. ...And I met my husband-to-be. No small thing. Fortunately, however, I have learned to be more patient over time. I am not in such a hurry to get things done, to move on to the next room, to keep coloring over my past.

This chapter is about finding fresh perspective. It is also about painting over your past life and giving it a new glow. When I talk about coloring my world, I am not talking about surface appeal, I am actually referring to deeper, more soulful changes that actually shape the way we perceive things and act in the world. Such lasting, indelible changes come from spiritual, not physical, practices.

The eleventh step of the twelve-step program states: "Sought through prayer and meditation to improve our conscious contact with God as we understood Him ..."[22] Arlo Guthrie's words bear repeating here: "Bring your own God." This refers to God as *you* understand God, not someone else's image. Finding that God, developing a relationship with that Divine Power, is a very personal thing. My journey toward seeking God has led me into new areas in my life. One of them is yoga.

In my yoga class, my teacher often speaks of the chakras and the energy we derive from them. Initially, the mention of that word, "chakras," turned me off. It all sounded so New Age, and I tend to rebel against anything that smacks of a fad even, sometimes, to my detriment. My feelings were affirmed by my work in the bookstore, where books on the chakras sat next to those on crystals and witchcraft. My rigid mind scoffed at the suggestion that any of those areas might actually provide healing. But I reminded myself that those who doubt are those who never tried something different. It is important to keep an open mind. So, I began to dip my toes into the world of the chakras, albeit tentatively.

What I found blew my mind.

The chakras, which have been around for thousands of years but which have only been utilized in the West for a very short time, are energy centers found in every human body. They are located in the front and back of the human spine. What does this all have to do with coloring my world? It just so happens that every chakra—and there are seven of them—has its own color and its own specific vibration frequency. Number one is red, two is orange, three is yellow, four is green, five is blue, six is indigo, and seven is violet or white. Yes, the colors of the rainbow! In meditation, I visualize the chakra's energy as liquid light enfolding my body, and in doing so, I align myself with my Creator. I don't pretend to be an expert in this energy rainbow, but I will share with you some of my experience in working with the various chakras.

Following my open mind, I allowed myself to engage in conversation with these pockets of energy. Through meditation, I immersed myself in the colored light that one or another emanated. I found myself drawn at first to the third chakra (yellow) which is located at the center of the solar plexus. According to Ernesto Ortiz, author of *The Akashic Records*, the third chakra is "the seat of the emotions and connects feeling with personal will. It is the seat of focus, decision, volition, and willpower. When this chakra is balanced, the person feels confident, decisive, focused and committed to his or her path."[23] Initially, I chose to meditate on this chakra because I love the color yellow. If I had to be bathed in light, I preferred that it be yellow. I soon realized, through my work with this chakra, that my desire to continue on the path I have chosen greatly benefited from my immersing myself in the third chakra. I found I had more confidence, more belief in myself, a greater sense of purpose and commitment to my goals. I wore the yellow light like a shawl around my shoulders; it encouraged me all day long.

When I feel my third chakra energy begin to list out of balance, I turn to the fourth chakra (green), the Heart Chakra. This chakra connects me to balance, patience, kindness, generosity, peace, humor, and forgiveness. When I meditate on this chakra, I imagine myself lying in a field of new grass or looking up at the green umbrella of a leafy tree. Green always smells to me like the Earth after rain. Fecund. It is a calm color, the color of life. No wonder I find it so soothing, so comforting. When I open myself to this chakra, I find I can open my heart to others more freely, and that is always a good thing.

The other chakras—each with their own colors and energy—have a place and purpose. I call on them intermittently, though the third and fourth chakras are the two I visit most often. I recommend you play with the chakras. Play with meditation. Even if you don't choose to use these energy centers as your guide, there are many ways to meditate that facilitate a connection with the Higher Power.

Coloring the world through meditating on the chakras is an illuminating, energizing practice. Meditation changes perception, erases negative thinking, encourages growth and imagination, and manifests peace. While I consider myself somewhat of a dilettante in meditation, I do find it to be an intensely practical and useful way to bring new colors into my life, to lead me forward on my path of self-transformation.

ॐ

Leaving the esoteric aside, what about painting as a way of giving our remodeled life a fresh glow? When you think about it, we have done all the spiritual prep work. We have scraped and spackled our pasts as we have become truthful with ourselves about just who we are and what needs fixing. We have taken the time, patiently, to mull over the paint swatches at the hardware store, choosing those colors that suit not just us but those we live with. We have taken our time, done our homework, and not forced the painting project forward.

But wait! Doesn't that sound a little bit like procrastination? I have to ask myself, *Why have I put off painting the front door? Why has it taken forever to paint the brown trim blue?* Or more significantly, *Why am I sitting with all those paints and easels in my closet, not lifting a brush?* This then leads to questions like, *Why have I left that feature film on my computer, never sending it out? Why have I stopped tracking my food? Why have I stopped stepping on the scale? Why have I not communicated with my sister in years? What happened to praying?*

Sometimes I put off "painting" my life, applying a new fresh coat of color (or calling my sisters, praying, and stepping on that damn scale), because I am lazy. I want someone else to do the work for me. When painting a house, you can always hire a professional to do the job. But painting a life? Applying that coat of whatever it is that is going to make me stand out in a crowd as authentically myself? That is often a hard thing to do. Fear gets in the way. Fear, with his band of bullies: Expectations, Doubts, and Pride.

So, first of all, what am I afraid of? With my writing, my number one fear is not being any good, being judged a fraud. I was told when I was in sixth grade that I was not a good writer. Every day, at the end of classes, when the other students were out playing field hockey or lacrosse in the fresh air, I was stuck in a stuffy classroom with Miss Wagner and her standard poodle, Zoot. Miss Wagner, with her onion breath and enormous breasts, would lean over me, insisting I diagram sentence after sentence, as though such an ability would make a writer of me. But I had to do it or I would fail.

Around that same time, I wrote a poem that I wanted to enter in the school writing competition. My mother told me it was bad and had my older sister, the *real* poet and writer, write one *for* me, which I submitted. It won, of course, under my name, and the message was tattooed on my soul: *You're a no-good writer. Fraud.* These kinds of thoughts are my "go-to" place when I have any success; I believe I'm going to be found out. I'll be stripped of all my medals, ridiculed in the streets, shamed, so I had better not try.

… To which I say, "Bullshit!" That was then. This is now. We all have a right to a voice, and I had a voice then. Despite the naysayers, I won the Lower School English Prize that year for my short story "Sea Change," a little piece about our St. Bernard, Nana, who was killed by a car.

჻

Another bully that, like Fear, tries to stop me from applying a new fresh coat of paint to my life is Expectations. This is such a mean, pernicious bully, and confusing too. We are told in our culture that we should set goals, go for the brass ring, market our brands, make the sale. The expectation is, if we are going to be counted as successes, we must achieve certain levels, hold a certain weight, make a specific amount of money. What all those expectations don't take into consideration is the element of surprise, the magic that comes from not knowing, turning the corner and suddenly seeing what is there. If I live my life in a state of expectation, I will be living a life of disappointment. I don't choose to color my world in negativity and stress today. I prefer to let go of expectations and be surprised by joy.

Doubt, a third old bully, may at first seem like a doddering old fogey, clearing his throat repeatedly and reminding you to be careful lest you falter. But Doubt, with his twin sister Pride, can really create havoc in a life. On the one hand, Doubt feeds into all the bad messages I tell myself: *I'm no good. I can't do it. They hate me. No one will come. I am such a liar.* While Doubt drowns in the quicksand of self-loathing, Pride pulls at him to get out. *Doesn't he know how special I am?* my Pride brain asks. *I am better than most of the other people here. I deserve for everyone to support me. They are fools if they don't. I'll show them.*

While these two are tugging at the corners of my soul, I am trying to stay balanced. I paint over their depression and egotism with a calming gray called Ullswater Mist. All I want is to walk on the fells (English hills) in summer where I visited as a young teen. Or in the English moors, knee-high in purple heather, among the fat, shaggy ponies that graze peacefully. Those were some happy memories. So, I apply a coat of paint over and over, until all the screeching voices are gone.

TOOLKIT #10

FIND THE RIGHT GIZMOS. The obvious tool for painting a house would be a set of good brushes, but I find that the more necessary tool is the little metal gizmo the hardware store provides to open the can. Without that tool, nothing can happen. In recovery terms, Courage is like that. Without Courage, it is impossible to move forward in transforming. There are too many obstacles that want to derail us, too many trials too heavy to bear. Without Courage, we would fall by the wayside, losing our way. The following tools are the elements of Courage that have sustained me on my journey.

LISTEN TO YOUR IMAGINATION. My imagination fuels me. It provides the reason for my continued growth. I see others further down the road than me, and I can imagine being as composed, compassionate, and gentle as they are. Using Shakti Gawain's lead, I can visualize myself as a new being, reborn in a new life.

When I read the ninth step promises in the twelve-step recovery programs, I can imagine comprising those ideals:

"If we are painstaking about this phase of our development, we will be amazed before we are halfway through. We are going to know a new freedom and a new happiness ...." 22

"A new freedom and a new happiness."[24] These are not extravagant promises. I have seen them come true in many other people's lives, as well as my own. For me, at the beginning of my journey, freedom and happiness were the brass rings for which I strived; they kept me going when things got tough. Because I could imagine these goals coming true in my life, I set my course for them, taking and carrying out suggestions that would lead them to be manifested in my life. Specifically, I was encouraged to attend ninety twelve-step meetings in ninety days, to get a sponsor to guide me through the program, and to abstain from drinking or using any mind-altering substance, no matter what the situation.

And to seek a Power greater than myself.

Without my imagination, I would have floundered like "a boat with a furled sail at rest in a harbor." However, my imagination "lift[ed] the sail / And [let me] catch the winds of destiny," as Edgar Lee Masters wrote in his *Spoon River Anthology*.[25] I believe it was my destiny, for example, for me to approach a major bookstore to launch my first book, because that query led me to meet the manager who then hired me as a bookseller. While working there, I came up with the idea for this book, which my manager suggested I share with my current publisher. So, here we are. Today, all those promises have happened— and keep happening—for me.

I am living a life beyond my wildest dreams.

HAVE PATIENCE. Patience plays an important role in any life. Without patience, I would lose my incentive to keep going in spite of drought and disaster. Patience allows me to surrender, to wait, to watch life unfold. It makes the miraculous possible. Patience removes stress and anxiety, allowing the imagination to play without the pressure of exhausting expectations or unreasonable demands. While I wait, I have the opportunity to learn about myself and the world around me. Patience is a great teacher and can be a good friend.

BE PERSISTENT. My transformation would not have been possible without my almost stubborn persistence. When told I could *not, I did.* When I was told I had debilitating handicaps, I challenged myself. When faced with new obstacles, I made my way through. I like to say I was "stuck like a dope with a thing called hope."[26] I still am. I feel fortunate in having been given that name.

Still, hoping is not enough. Courage and persistence take action, and the balance between waiting and acting is a delicate one. I am reminded of the line from the song "The Gambler," made famous by Kenny Rogers, "You've got to know when to hold 'em, know when to fold 'em."[27]

In my relentless pursuit of God, I had to learn how to quiet down and simply be in order to experience the Divine Presence. In chasing after my writing career, I have had to learn how to let things percolate and unfold, while at the same time picking up my pen and practicing my craft daily. I need to practice punching and kickboxing, not so I can go around doing martial arts all day, but so I will have those skills when I need them ... if I need them. I need to keep my commitments to myself to take my medication, eat properly, and exercise so when life hands me a curveball like a deadly virus and I—or someone I love—falls ill, my body and soul will be ready to stand up to the stress.

"Nevertheless, she persisted."[28] And because she—and all the other women and men who passionately believed in something bigger than themselves—persisted, the change that allowed her to take on a new way of living occurred. That change *is* occurring today. No change will ever come unless we persist in doing what we know is the next right thing for us to do. It's very personal. It's universal. It takes courage to save a life, a world.

And remember: there is no rest for the weary ... but there *are* naps.

CHAPTER 11
The Swing in The Backyard

Whenever I pass by a house that has a treehouse, or a playset, or a swing in the backyard, I smile. The presence of this play equipment tells me there is something fun going on. The house, no matter how beautifully updated and restored, doesn't take itself too seriously. No matter whether there are children living in the house or not, a swing or glider in the backyard is a sign that the people who live in the home know how to relax, to take time out from life just to play.

I keep photographs under a glass panel on top of my desk. They are pictures of my kids when they were young, tan, and smiling on Martha's Vineyard, and one of my younger daughter walking on the beach in Thailand. There are others too, but one of my favorites is a little snapshot of myself as a kid, probably only two years old, with white-blonde hair and chubby legs. I am wearing a white sundress and sitting on a swing, looking content and dreamy. Enjoying life.

What would all this home remodeling work be for if it weren't to enjoy oneself?

This need for enjoyment is equally true of remodeling a life. Speaking for myself, I haven't gone through decades of self-transformation just to end up a sour, disgruntled old woman. Far from it. I am here to have a good time, and to share my good time with others. But it hasn't always been that way.

చి

When I got sober, in 1981, I was broken. Terrified. I had no idea how I was going to climb out of the hole I had dug for myself with my drinking. Friends in the twelve-step program told me, "It's easy. Just let go and let God." That's all very well if you understand what that means, but I had no clue how to "let go."

"Let go of what?" I asked, my fists clenched, my jaw locked. And as for "letting God," I had given up on God a long time ago. Or at least I believed God had given up on *me*. Despite my reservations, I stayed away from alcohol, took suggestions from people with more sobriety than I had, and worked on developing a relationship with a God of my understanding. I read books, plenty of books, thinking they were where I would get my answers. Some of them were quite helpful. I went back to church. I found a place that suited me, with a rector, a Michigan alum, named "Moose." And I prayed. But I felt a scant connection with Power outside myself.

By my second anniversary in the program, I had inklings that *something* was at work. I was still sober, my life had smoothed out, and I was even starting to repair relationships that had gone awry. Still, my connection with God felt shallow and unconvincing.

So, one day, I fell to my knees in my living room and I started to plead with God to reveal Himself to me. When I say "plead," I might as well say "bleed." I poured my heart and soul out, yelling at the ceiling, pounding the floor. I was weeping and wailing, not concerned about what the neighbors might think. This went on for quite a while until, suddenly, I yawned. A great, big, fat baby yawn. That got my attention.

"Oh, heavens," I thought, "God must be bored with me."

Just then, a voice came out of nowhere, clear as day. It said, "Run along and play."

It was then I found my solution: Play. Stop taking life so seriously. Get my head out of the books and the brain, and move into my heart. Run by the river and watch the ducks stick their asses in the air while the diamonds skip along the water. Breathe in the cool spring breezes. Laugh.

～

My fallback, all my life, had been to brood, to engage in deep, philosophical ruminations, to write poems, even as a child, about death and existence. On one level, the grown-ups were impressed that I, as an eight-year-old, could practically discuss *King Lear* and Kierkegaard. But from my perspective, it was a burden. I grew up faster than I should have, skipping those magical years of spontaneity. My sisters used to call me "Old Yeller," teasing that I was "so ripe, I would fall off the vine." When others rubbed their hands in thick finger paints, I colored deliberately inside the lines of my coloring book. At Christmas, when we decorated cookies, I cringed as my little sisters poured sprinkles indiscriminately; my Red Hots were lined up like little soldiers.

I was all about control, from an early age, probably because I felt so out-of-control inside. The idea of no boundaries, no rules, no edge to the Universe terrified me. It wasn't until I started drinking that I could enjoy a good romp in the fields, a raucous chorus of Beatle songs.

I remember some of our childhood games. In retrospect, they seemed to me to be not so much for fun, but rather metaphors for life. "Stuck in the Mud" captured how I felt: out of control, stuck in the muddy uncertainty of my own existence. I wanted to break free but was dependent on someone else to liberate me. Little did I know that this would be the story of my life. Since then, I have had one "angel" after another free me from my bondage *du jour*. But, of course, God has been the Great Liberator, rescuing me time and time again.

Another popular game was "Red Rover," in which the Rover calls specific groups to try to make it past her to home base. This game, which should have been entertaining, if a little scary, filled me with anxiety. What if I were chosen? How would I escape certain death? The race was on to figure out the perfect route to base, because nothing less than perfection was acceptable. And if I weren't chosen, what would that mean? That I had already died in everyone's eyes, that I didn't matter, that I had ceased to exist? Pretty grim thoughts for a young girl, but they were mine.

Everything I thought and did from a young age on was colored by an alphabet of monsters: Abandonment, Bravado, Competition, Dread, Embarrassment, Fear. ... Shall I go on? The monsters children have under their beds? Mine lived in my *head*, creating a filter that cast a dark light on the world and took the joy out of everything.

At what point did winning at everything become all important? At what point did happiness become something I felt I needed to earn, but that no amount of striving could buy? At what point did life become too serious for words, causing me to turn to pills, razor blades, and the bottle? No one incident stands out as that pivotal moment. There were so many signs along the way. The point at which I started drinking on a regular basis, in my early teens. The blackouts. The hiding booze. The unpredictable behavior once I took that first drink. The moment when I began to slide downhill, and yet those closest to me still thought I was all right.

And I was, on one level.

჻

I am sure you have heard stories about kids like me, teenagers who excelled at everything. I was a high-honors student; I played on several varsity athletic teams; I sang in the school choir and served on the altar guild; I was an accomplished actress. On my graduation day, I won the majority of prizes given out at school. I was blonde and pretty. To all accounts, I was "having fun."

There is a saying that I love: "Never judge your insides by other people's outsides." To those who have ever felt jealous of my success, my life, I say, "Just take a look inside." My years as a teenager and into my twenties were years of *Hell.* I sometimes fool myself into thinking that they weren't all that bad. After all, I was thin, and in my junior year of high school, I fell in love. But honestly, I had already started drinking daily by the time I was about fourteen years old, and things went downhill from there. My progression into alcoholism was a landslide greased by manic-depression.

And the thing that pushed me over the edge was meeting "X" and falling in love at the age of fifteen.

I call him "X" because, I believe now, he could have been anybody. It just happened that the stars aligned and I fell for his green eyes on first sight. I pity that poor soul who stepped into my line of vision and became the object of my desire. In retrospect, I see that I went into a manic state the day I met him and cycled through depression and mania for many years after he had left me for another girl.

In the early days of our relationship, there was no fun. There was just this acute need on my part to love, and be loved by, him. To earn his affection, I starved myself into anorexia. To prove he could not hurt me, I let him put a match to my flesh and burn my hand until it blistered. My "love" for him was totally one-sided— an obsession, really—though he strung me along with occasional calls and visits. Once, we took a trip to his sister's up North. Another time, a surprise visit when I was working as a mother's helper on Block Island. While I was busy visualizing our babies and picking out names, he was sending me lyrics to Bonnie Raitt songs about break-ups. I couldn't hear them, however; I was too far gone. I was drinking excessively, daydreaming addictively, and isolating from everyone in my life.

If this is what love looks like, I'll take it, I thought to myself ... and then cried some more into my wine.

That boy left me, which was a good thing for him. I didn't really love him. I loved the *idea* of him. He just reinforced for me the difficult truth that life sucked. In my mind, it was obvious that we were all just put on this earth to suffer and die. With X's departure, any vestige of "play" that I'd had in me disappeared. I resigned myself instead to a life of disappointment, depression, and resentment. Like sugar to cancer, that choice nourished my alcoholism, which flared up and razed my life.

Things became much worse in my life between 1976 and getting sober in 1981. I remember going to a bar at that time with my first husband. We lived in Cambridge, Massachusetts, and would drink in Harvard Square. On our way home, several blocks to Linnaean Street, we would stop for a nightcap at another bar. One night as I sat at our table, nursing my wine, I looked over at a woman who sat at the bar. She was draped over the man next to her, her lipstick smeared, hair disheveled. She looked like one of the whores from a Toulouse-Lautrec painting. I guessed she was probably in her early forties. The sad thing was, I, in my early twenties at the time, felt just the way she looked. Sadder still, I could not imagine enduring life until I turned forty; I was sure I would be dead before then.

~

So how did I rise from the ashes? I listened to the voice that came to me much later that one day in 1982 as I prayed: "Run along and Play!" I would be dishonest if I told you that as soon as I received the message, I started channeling Jimmy Buffet and booked a cruise to Nowhere. It simply was not that easy, because, truth be told, I had completely forgotten *how* to play, to relax and enjoy life. First of all, there was no more booze in my system, so sitting back and admiring a sunset was almost impossible for me. Second, if I were to play, I had to be moving. And I mean *moving:* fifteen-mile runs by the Charles River; twenty-five-mile bike rides in the Sourland Mountains. Everything was overdone, overblown. Nothing was simple.

There was, too, the reality that my bipolar disorder was, as yet, undiagnosed and untreated. So, whatever I did for fun, I did over the top. Or not at all. When our children had birthdays, I threw parties that would rival a Roman feast. In 1993, when the theme for my son's third birthday was knights, I ordered a cake the size of a small castle. I had my husband handcraft swords, helmets, and shields. I seem to recall that we found a small pony for rides, though I may be making that up in my mind. Whatever it was, we were not wealthy, by any means, and yet I insisted we celebrate to the max, no matter what the cost. Did the kids have fun? Sure, they did, chasing one another around like gladiators. Did I have fun? Not so much. Mainly, I was tired, just as I always was after orchestrating some party or holiday so that it appeared perfect. And fun. When in actuality, it wasn't much fun at all.

ॐ

In 1998, when I discovered *The Artist's Way*, and simultaneously began treatment for bipolar disorder, I started to get a glimpse of what fun could look like. It looked an awful lot like starting to love myself. In the book, Julia Cameron encourages the reader to make an Artist's Date with herself once a week. Nothing fancy, just an hour or two doing something fun by oneself. As one who had never really engaged in fun without all the shitty filters that accompanied it, I found this to be a most difficult exercise indeed. Still, I persevered.

Here are some of the things I have done for play over the years:

- taken a photo safari at the park
- visited an art gallery
- walked to the bakery and bought a pastry
- sat in an empty church and listened to the silence
- attended a free concert on the green
- watched a movie I knew my husband wouldn't like
- taken a bubble bath
- treated myself to a mani-pedi

- written poems
- bought sushi for lunch, and eaten
  it in the sunshine
- made collages
- baked something delicious
- bought myself flowers,
  or picked ones from my garden
- created a mosaic stepping stone
- planted a perennial garden and a window box

The list could go on. The point is, I learned, through taking these Artist's Dates, that I *do* know how to play. I do know how to have fun by myself, and I am always learning how to have fun with others.

Actually, I've realized that I almost always have more fun when I am around others than when I am by myself. This is a far cry from the way I used to be as a young girl and even as a middle-aged woman. In the past, I always preferred Solitaire and crossword puzzles to games with other people, because I felt such a high level of competitiveness that took all the *fun* out of the fun. But I don't feel that way anymore. I know I don't have to win. I know I can play by myself, and I have a good time on my own, but I also know I love sharing moments of pleasure with other people.

⁊

On our recent trip to Arizona, my pleasure in seeing the fields brimming with golden poppies, and the blue and white flowers interspersed in the gold, would have been diminished had my daughter not been there with me. Her joy in every blossom, her delight in taking pictures of the smallest bloom, gave me such pleasure too. We passed my camera back and forth, each taking photos of moments we felt were most beautiful, laughing and enjoying the amazing scene.

The thing about this daughter is, she seems to get me. She knows what I will enjoy, in Nature and beyond. We are on the same wavelength as far as most music goes; she is totally clued in to what I like to eat; and she gives the most thoughtful, spot-on presents in the world. Once, not long ago, she gave me a gold bracelet with "Never Give Up" on it. I took that to heart. She is an easy person to play with. She is also an amazing woman in her own right. An adventuress, a humanitarian, a loyal friend, a brilliant artist, she has the most beautiful way of being in this world—loving it with her whole heart. Since she was little, she has exuded a positive, charismatic energy that makes me want to play along.

My other children display the same kind of energy, though they each have their own unique way of playing with me. For my son, we take long walks, discussing budding writing projects or finding new recipes to explore in the kitchen. He is my gentle companion, thoughtful and compassionate, the one who surprises me with flowers. The one who keeps me grounded in reality.

Of the three, my youngest daughter reminds me most of myself. Like her older sister, she is both artistic and cerebral, but she also keeps her toes (always carefully colored) in today. She is an extremely hard worker, an enthusiastic pet lover. She follows through on commitments, and is just insecure enough to remain humble. And she likes to shop! We have fun. We have developed a tradition of attending The Nutcracker ballet every Christmas season. She is the one who will keep the spirit of Christmas alive in our family when I am long gone.

I have fun with all of my children and feel so blessed they are in my life. I can't imagine a world without them.

Others? Not always so much. Be careful who you choose as your playmate. Or at least be mindful of the ways in which they can and cannot play with you. My husband and I have spent many happy hours and miles hiking all over the North and Southwest. We would love to hike Hadrian's Wall in northern England and up to Machu Picchu. In that regard, we are good playmates for each other. When we turn on the television, however, we definitely have our differences. For the lion's share of our thirty years together, I have indulged him in his shoot 'em up, blood and guts, science fiction stuff while foregoing those shows I would prefer. Fortunately, I don't really care that much for television anyway, so it's not a big deal.

When it comes to movies, however, there are many I haven't seen that I think I would have enjoyed. So what has kept me from going to the movies alone? Are there rules about playing, and going to the movies alone doesn't count as play? Well, no, but when I think about driving to the movies and watching something by myself, I feel hollow. I think that is because there are some ways we prefer to play alone and some ways we don't.

The important thing is to play. Don't take oneself too seriously. If something you are contemplating leaves you feeling hollow and sad, don't do it, no matter how "playful" it may seem to someone else. On the other hand, if something excites you, go do it! Go buy a dozen eggs and some food coloring and celebrate Easter, even if it is October. Get an ice cream cone in December and light a fire in May. It's all right. Be a rule breaker like those little kids who dress themselves for school and look like they just stepped out of all nine departments in a store. Who says shoes have to match? Who says buttons can't go in the back? Stripes and polka dots? Perfect. Play! Let loose! Be who you want to be and not who you have thought you were all your life. There's more to your story than meets your eye.

꙳

The most important thing I can do for my recovery is to play. Play keeps me present in the moment; play keeps me mindful of what I am doing. It keeps me out of people's hair and in my own little halo of self.

Rediscovering my inner Hopie has been one of the greatest joys of my life. People say that when I talk about the things I love—Nature, music, photography, hiking, meditation, food, sleep—I glow. I am reminded of Toll House cookies warm from my childhood neighbor's oven and hot cocoa steaming from her mugs. It is not me glowing. It is Love glowing through each of those things and the immense joy they have brought and continue to bring me.

TOOLKIT #11

PLAY. I believe it is only when we allow ourselves to be children again that we are in touch with the Divine Spark that created all things and makes us who we are. That little girl on the swing in her white sundress is the me I will always cherish. She is the me—Hopie—that I rediscovered as I remodeled my life.

Have fun! You have a choice to be happy or miserable. Choose joy!

REMEMBER: LIFE IS NOT A CHORE. My dear friend, Keith Jennison, reminded me frequently, in my youth, that life is not a problem to be solved, but rather a mystery to be enjoyed. Life is not unending misery. If I have learned anything in this life, it is that I have choices. I can choose sorrow, or I can choose happiness. It's all up to me.

But what of the person who suffers from PTSD or chronic depression? I say, look closely at the choices they are making on a daily basis. Are they eating nourishing food? Are they getting adequate sleep? Exercise? Are they drinking at least a liter of water a day? Are they taking their medication? Have they read something uplifting lately? Practiced affirmations? Called a friend? Walked in Nature? If they are doing all these things, honestly, and still don't experience joy in their lives, then I don't know what to say. Those tools always work for me. Perhaps it would be a good time to seek professional help.

REMEMBER: HAPPINESS IS A CHOICE. Every morning when I wake up, I say a happiness prayer from Joseph Murphy's, *The Power of Your Subconscious Mind.*[29] It reminds me that I am not alone in the Universe, I am surrounded by Divine Love, and I am a spiritual magnet drawing good, positive energy toward myself. I say this. I believe this, and because I believe it, it manifests. I make the decision to be happy every day ... and it works.

DON'T TAKE YOURSELF TOO SERIOUSLY. What stands in the way of the play-filled life? You have seen it, the mothers who fuss over their children playing in the dirt or holding a baby chick, making the child scrub her hands until they are raw and then dousing them in hand sanitizer. Where's the fun in that? It used to be that if a child hadn't ingested at least a cup of dirt a day, he hadn't played. Gone are the days of eating raw chocolate-chip cookie dough. Of trick or treating without strict parental supervision. Of wandering in the woods, alone. No one knows how to play anymore! Since when did life become all about political correctness, sanitation, and digitalization? Some children will only know a lilac if they see it in a role playing game; they'll never smell the heady lavender blossoms or taste a crisp green bean fresh from the vine. They won't feel the hot juice of a cherry tomato from the garden spill down their chins.

It's time to get dirty, I say, to pick up fat earthworms in our muddy fingers. To make a mess in the kitchen concocting playdough. To have tea parties in laurel blossoms. It is time to stop being so prissy about everything, stop taking ourselves so seriously, and start enjoying the precious disruption of creating.

Adults are especially good at taking themselves too seriously. They hide behind important titles and degrees, transactions and mergers. Everything they see is in dollar signs. But where are the dollar signs in a meadow of wildflowers? What price would you pay to be as wild and free as the Outer Banks ponies? Who has more power than the hawk, gliding over the tree line? You cannot pay for that liberty, that beauty. Look at the little foxes playing in the snow. Can you be as silly as that? To all those grown-ups who believe a job, money, and security are everything, I cry—you guessed it—*"Bullshit!"*

My husband and I have lived on very little for a number of years now, and yet we have never wanted for anything. No, we don't have a fancy house and cars and vacations, but we do have a lovely piece of Heaven we call our own. We have found ways to play without much and to truly enjoy life.

Happiness doesn't have a price tag; it is a lifestyle.

I can be happy if I don't take myself too seriously.

NO EXPECTATIONS. One of the most magical things about play is its randomness. I think that is why I like writing, because I am never exactly sure what the pen is going to put down on paper next. Poems twist. Novels turn. Screenplays jump off the page and leap around the room. Even memoirs, predictable as they might seem, frequently leap out of the dark and surprise the shit out of me! To rein in play, to give it perimeters and rules, is self-defeating. You might as well tell Marc Chagall to paint between the lines. No more dreamy, blue cows floating in space or wedding couples lying, large as a house, on top of a small hill.

Of course, there is a place for games—soccer, football, baseball, tennis, and such—all must have their rules and regulations. Even games like Hide and Seek, Capture the Flag, and Tag follow a prescribed plan. But that is not the sort of play I am talking about. I am talking about the Maria von Trapp kind of play when she is on the mountaintop, arms flung wide, singing at the top of her lungs about how alive the hills are with music. I get chills even thinking about that scene, so wild it is with joy. On my good days, I surrender myself to that kind of play, when I am cooking something new in the kitchen or planting perennials in my garden. My favorite way to play is to spontaneously take off down the beach, racing against the waves, or fall down in deep snow, fanning my arms like angel wings. The point is, when I am playing, truly playing, with Life as my only companion, I am fully engaged in the moment, living without any expectations at all.

In Dante Alighieri's masterpiece, *The Divine Comedy*, the sign over the gates to Hell read: "ABANDON HOPE, ALL YE WHO ENTER HERE."[30] I would like to rewrite that for the skeptics who think that such spontaneous, carefree play should be left to children. "ABANDON DOUBT, ALL YE WHO QUESTION THIS."

There is no question in my mind that actively engaging in play takes away the need for any expectations at all.

HEAL. Genuine play is one of the most restorative, peace-making activities in the world. I believe if people would take themselves a little less seriously, remove the sticks from their backsides, and allow themselves to play for a good hour every day, the Universe would heal. Blow bubbles, not bombs! If we all did this, we humans would come to realize our true place on this planet: we are not here to change it or one another, to concretize every landscape, to pollute every body of water, though we seem as a species to be pretty good at doing those things. We are here to *play* with the Earth, with all creation. To flit as the butterflies and bees, landing on pillows of pollen and sucking the sweetness out of them. To lie in the shade of some magnificent tree like a golden lioness, ever-patient, watching as her cubs roll in the dirt. To float on our backs in the bubbling water, like an otter whose little pink toes peek out into the air. We have been given the ultimate playground, and yet we have chosen to pulverize it. Playing in it may help us all heal.

When you actually experience the awesomeness of the Grand Canyon, the Saguaro National Park, the Outer Banks, Alaska, the Everglades, from sea to shining sea—the wonder of our country alone, let alone the rest of the world—it becomes difficult, if not impossible, not to take steps to stop drilling, prevent fracking, minimize plastic usage, regulate pesticides. People today are so focused on how fragile *they* are, scarred by experiences of youth. What about the planet? She is scarred too, but has no voice to articulate her pain.

My husband and I visited the Joyce Kilmer Memorial Forest, here in North Carolina to stand among the ancient trees. I hugged one and spoke to it as if it were a friend. I photographed the bark and lichen, tulip-tree leaves and girth. I was very small next to one of these giant fellows. This is what they taught me:

STILL STANDING

Ancient trees,
broader than the span
of my husband's outstretched arms,
taller than the top of the canopy
into which they disappear
up toward Heaven,

stand like sentinels in the forest.
I press my hand against their rough bark,
thick with grooves and pocks,
say a little prayer.
I hear nothing back,
only the heavy message that they have been
in this forest a long, long time.
Long before I learned to walk and wander,
they mastered the secret of standing still.
If they could walk away now,
lumbering, gigantic,
shaking the Earth with every step,
would they?
These trees, content where they are
nestled among mountain streams, ferns,
pale white rhododendron, whisper
Why move when where you are is so perfect?[31]

When I spend time playing—whether in Nature or out—
I heal.

CHAPTER 12
The New House

The process of remodeling a home can be expensive, exhausting, and often frustrating. There are months when the kitchen is being redone, for example, where your dishes, pots and pans, glasses, mugs, cutlery, and china are packed away in boxes and shoved behind the Christmas decorations in the basement. You eat out more, gain weight, and grow grumpy with the frequent delays. When the wrong cabinets come in and you have to send out for new ones, another six weeks go by and you are ready to tear your hair out. Remodeling is never as seamless as reality television would lead you to believe. Whose reality is it that shows the process, which really takes several months if not more, stuffed into an hour-long segment? Intellectually, you know it can't be so, it won't be that easy, but the promise nevertheless lingers.

In truth, any kind of remodeling takes at least three times as long as you expect it to. There is a rule of thumb that states it takes ninety days to change a habit. Three months. At least. This is true also of both remodeling a house and remodeling a life. So, what does that mean to us? Should we not proceed? Should we not make the changes that are going to improve our quality of life? Hell, no! "Bring it on," I say, just be prepared for a slow and steady process.

Then, at last, comes the conclusion. Suddenly, one day, you find yourself walking into your kitchen a month after the builders have left. All the dishes have been put into their proper places. The glassware sparkles through the new glass cupboard doors. Your favorite mug, now visible, beckons you to make a cup of tea. You sit in the comfy chair in the breakfast nook, a space that was never there before the renovation, and look out at this new creation. Gleaming, fresh, inviting—all these positive words pop into your mind. Looking at the little blue vase filled with daffodils that sits on the countertop, you sigh. Peace. That is what all the hardship of remodeling has brought you. Another chapter has come to a close.

Peace.

꙳

When I look back on the decades during which my life has been under construction (and still is today), I marvel that I didn't just give up, walk into the ocean, and never come back. There were times when life was so painful, so heavy, I thought I couldn't bear its weight. But I kept going, one step at a time. I had heard the message, "Stick around until the miracle happens," so I did, waiting for the miracle to occur. Of course, miracles were occurring all the time, I just couldn't always see them.

I didn't know then what "The Miracle" would look like, but I think I know now. It is the miracle of sobriety. The miracle of a marriage that stayed together. The miracle of three amazing children. The miracle of family and friends. And this is just the beginning.

The Miracle is how I absolutely trust that the Universe is a safe, loving place where there is enough for everyone. It is a place where I am looked after and taken care of every minute, and I don't have to worry, fret, or push anymore. It is the belief that I have in myself all that I need to be happy in any circumstance, to succeed in all efforts, and to accept setbacks graciously as a necessary part of life. In my Miracle Life, there are no chance encounters. Nothing is either too small to warrant my attention or too vast to overwhelm it.

There is a reason for all things.

My Miracle may not be your miracle. You may think I am just blowing hot air, but my life has taken on a flow of its own. I ride on the back of my Higher Power who delights in all things good. Mine is a wonderful life, and I hope the tools I have shared with you in this little book help you to find your Miracle too. I feel free to sit in my comfy chair and look around at my remodeled life. So shiny, so fresh, so inviting. All the hard work it took to get to this point has been worth it. Of course, the remodel is never over, the journey continues.

I will share with you another of my poems:

MIRACULOUS

Some see God as a stern judge
parsing out judgement,
arbitrary and unforgiving.
Not my God.
My God is an artist
with a tray of brilliant paints,
creating the zillions of bright things
put in my path every day.

Driving down the highway,
headed toward my daughter's home,
I see a cluster of weeds:
tall, mustard-colored goldenrod,
a burst of white asters,
frothy pink grass, soft as a whisper—
nothing that anyone planted.
Just God,
who knows better than to call names,
to segregate and divide.

God is a blizzard of possibilities,
a downpour of creativity,
God shines light in the darkest places,
finding beauty under rocks
and in the deepest seas.
Tenuous, milky mushrooms
shelved in a dark cave
as electric pink fish wiggle their antennae
on the ocean's floor.

I am so blessed to hold your hand
whoever you are,
whatever color, race, religion, sex,
to walk with you on this path,
enfolded in miracles,
and call this place ours.
Our world,
God's world.
An impossible Universe brought to life,
throbbing with Love.

Epilogue

Thank you for reading this book. When I set out to write *How to Remodel a Life* and to share my story with you, my goal was to create something that would give people Hope. (No pun intended.) My life, fraught with difficulty for many years, has been transformed into what I can only describe as an oasis of serenity. Of course, I have my ups and downs. That is just part of the human condition. The difference is, today I have stopped fighting life. I am at peace, and I couldn't just keep this to myself. I was compelled to spread the message that if some simple steps are taken, anyone can enjoy such a life.

So, I sought to reach out—particularly to those who are suffering, as I believe we all are—with the message that there is a solution to such pain. If you have gleaned something from this book that will help you on your path, I have succeeded. Your journey toward becoming your true self is very important to me. I would love for you to share your story with me along the way. If you would like to get in touch with me, or to find out more about my work, please contact me at my website www.hopeandersen.org.

Whatever your path, remember: you are never too young to start the journey; you are never too old to ask for help; it is never too late to begin remodeling your life.

Peace,

Hope Andersen

Author's Note

Some months after completing this manuscript, I was diagnosed with third-stage kidney disease, the result in part due to taking lithium for so many years. My psychiatrist changed my medication and put me on one that filters through the liver rather than the kidneys. Still, there will be no going back. The disease cannot be reversed, only arrested. What comes after is either transplant, dialysis, or death.

When I received this news, I fell into a week of morbid reflection. But I have since climbed out of that hole by practicing just what I have written in these pages. I shared my situation with family and friends. I sought professional help. I practice affirmations. And I changed my way of eating and exercising to adjust to my new reality. So, a new chapter begins with new ways that I must take care of myself.

Not long after that, the face of the world changed with the onset of the coronavirus. Life for everyone on the planet suddenly required self-sacrifice and adjustment to a new way of life. We, as a species, have been forced to change our behavior if we are to survive. These are times of uncertainty and fear. But I believe that disease, whether in the individual or in the masses, presents us with the opportunity to exercise our right to live, to choose Life. I have found that practicing the suggestions in this book can help you through any adversity. Here is a final poem for you:

THE CONVERSATION

If I came face to face with God,
sitting this very minute
at our old wooden table
scarred and burned by casseroles and knives,
I might be inclined to be forward,
and tell Him not to be gentle with me—
there is no need.
But underneath my worn silk blouse
my heart would flutter
and I would plead,
Be kind, be kind.
I say I am not afraid
of Death.
It's losing Life that scares me.
Black void of no feeling,
no being, ceasing to exist.
Like the space in my mind
when I can't remember something.

I would miss blackberry cobbler hot from the oven;
hugs from my children
spring birds early in February,
breaking winter's shell;
purple violets embroidering the newly-green lawn.
This isn't over yet,
the conversation between us.

Endnotes

1. *Alcoholics Anonymous* (New York City, New York: Alcoholics Anonymous World Services, Inc., 1976)
2 Mary Oliver, "The Journey," in *Dream Work* (Boston, Massachusetts: Atlantic Monthly Press, 1986)
3 Richard Rogers and Oscar Hammerstein, "I Whistle a Happy Tune," in *The King and I* (Original Broadway Score, 1951)
4 "You Can Get Anything You Want at Alice's Restaurant," *Off the Path from New York to Boston.* (WSHU Public Radio, NPR News and Classical Music, November 22, 2019), https://www.wshu.org/post/you-can-get-anything-you-want-alices-restaurant#stream/0
5 Hope Andersen, "Lye Brook Falls," in *Taking in Air* (American Fork, Utah: Kelsey Books, Alabaster Leaves Publishing, 2018)
6 John Keats, "Ode on a Grecian Urn," Poetry Foundation (Poetry Foundation), accessed March 31, 2020, https://www.poetryfoundation.org/poems/44477/ode-on-a-grecian-urn
7 Pema Chödrön, *Comfortable with Uncertainty* (New York City, New York: Penguin Random House, 2003)
8 Dale Carnegie, *How to Stop Worrying and Start Living* (New York City, New York: Pocket Books, 1984)

9 Lawrence Block, *Writing the Novel from Plot to Print to Pixel* (LB Productions, 2016)

10 Lewis Carroll, *Alice in Wonderland* (London: The Children's Press, 1963)

11 Richard Le Gallienne, "I Meant to Do My Work Today," in *Collected Works of Richard Le Gallienne* (Charleston, South Carolina: BiblioBazaar, BiblioLife, 2007)

12 Mary Ann Hoberman, *A House Is a House for Me* (London: Penguin Books, 1972)

13 "Fast Facts," Centers for Disease Control and Prevention (US Department of Health and Human Services), accessed November 15, 2019, https://www.cdc.gov/tobacco/data_statistics/fact_sheets/fast_facts/index.htm

14 Mary Oliver, "The Summer Day," in *New and Selected Poems* (Boston, Massachusetts: Beacon Press, 1992)

15 *Twelve Steps and Twelve Traditions* (New York City, New York: Alcoholics Anonymous World Services, Inc., 1976)

16 Emily Dickinson, "We Play at Paste," in *The Complete Poems of Emily Dickinson* (New York City, New York: Back Bay Books, Hachette, 1976)

17 Chit Chat Farm was a part of the Caron Treatment Center in Wernersville, Pennsylvania.

18 William Wordsworth, "The World Is Too Much with Us," Poetry Foundation, accessed March 31, 2020, https://www.poetryfoundation.org/poems/45564/the-world-is-too-much-with-us

19 Don Miguel Ruiz, *The Four Agreements* (San Rafael, California: Amber-Allen Publishing, Inc. , 1997)

20 Dalai Lama, Desmond Tutu, and Douglas Carlton Adams, *The Book of Joy: Lasting Happiness in a Changing World* (New York City, New York: Avery, 2016)

21 Tenzin Gyatso, the Fourteenth Dalai Lama. "Compassion and the Individual," His Holiness the 14th Dalai Lama of Tibet (The Office of His Holiness the Dalai Lama), accessed March 31, 2020, https://www. dalailama.com/messages/compassion-and-human-values/compassion

22 *Twelve Steps and Twelve Traditions* (New York City, New York: Alcoholics Anonymous World Services, Inc., 1976)

23 Ernesto Ortiz, *The Akashic Records: Sacred Exploration of Your Soul's Journey Within the Wisdom of the Collective Consciousness* (Pompton Plains, New Jersey: New Page Books, The Career Press, 2015)

24 *Alcoholics Anonymous* (New York City, New York: Alcoholics Anonymous World Services, Inc., 1976)

25 Edgar Lee Masters, *Spoon River Anthology* (New York City, New York: Macmillan, 1966)

26 Richard Rogers and Oscar Hammerstein, "Stuck Like a Dope," in *South Pacific* (Original Broadway Score, 1949)

27 "The Gambler," *The Gambler* (United Artists Records, 1978, vinyl. Performed by Kenny Rogers, written by Don Schlitz. December, 1978)

28 Addison Mitchell McConnell, "Nevertheless, she persisted," Rebuke of Senator Elizabeth Warren (US Senate Debate for Confirmation of Senator Jeff Sessions, Washington, DC, February 7, 2017)

29 Joseph Murphy, *The Power of Your Subconscious Mind* (Radford, Virginia: Wilder Publications, 2007)

30 Dante Alighieri, "Canto 3," in *The Divine Comedy 1: Inferno* (New York City, New York: Penguin Classics, 2006)

31 Hope Andersen, "Still Standing," *The Awakenings Review*, forthcoming, 2020

Bibliography

Alcoholics Anonymous. New York City, New York:
Alcoholics Anonymous World Services, Inc., 1976.

Alighieri, Dante. "Canto 3." In *The Divine Comedy 1: Inferno.*
New York City, New York: Penguin Classics, 2006.

Andersen, Hope. "Lye Brook Falls." In *Taking in Air.*
American Fork, Utah: Kelsay Books, Alabaster Leaves
Publishing, 2018.

Andersen, Hope. "Still Standing." *The Awakenings Review,*
forthcoming, 2020.

Block, Lawrence. *Writing the Novel from Plot to Print to
Pixel.* LB Productions, 2016.

Carnegie, Dale. *How to Stop Worrying and Start Living.*
New York City, New York: Pocket Books, 1984.

Carroll, Lewis. *Alice in Wonderland.* London:
The Children's Press, 1963.

Chödrön, Pema. *Comfortable with Uncertainty.* New York
City, New York: Penguin Random House, 2003.

Dalai Lama, Desmond Tutu, and Douglas Carlton Abrams. *The Book of Joy: Lasting Happiness in a Changing World*. New York City, New York: Avery, 2016.

Dickinson, Emily. "We Play at Paste." In *The Complete Poems of Emily Dickinson*. New York City, New York: Back Bay Books, Hachette, 1976.

"Fast Facts." Centers for Disease Control and Prevention. US Department of Health and Human Services. Accessed November 15, 2019. https://www.cdc.gov/tobacco/data_statistics/fact_sheets/fast_facts/index.htm.

"The Gambler." *The Gambler*. United Artists Records, 1978, vinyl. Performed by Kenny Rogers, written by Don Schlitz. December, 1978.

Gyatso, Tenzin, the Fourteenth Dalai Lama. "Compassion and the Individual." His Holiness the 14th Dalai Lama of Tibet. The Office of His Holiness the Dalai Lama. Accessed March 31, 2020. https://www.dalailama.com/messages/compassion-and-human-values/compassion.

Hammerstein, Oscar, and Richard Rogers. "I Whistle a Happy Tune." In *The King and I*, Original Broadway Score, 1951.

Hammerstein, Oscar, and Richard Rogers. "Stuck Like a Dope." In *South Pacific*, Original Broadway Score, 1949.

Hoberman, Mary Ann. *A House Is a House for Me*. London: Penguin Books, 1972.

Keats, John. "Ode on a Grecian Urn." Poetry Foundation. Poetry Foundation . Accessed March 31, 2020. https://www.poetryfoundation.org/poems/44477/ode-on-a-grecian-urn.

Le Gallienne, Richard. "I Meant to Do My Work Today." In *Collected Works of Richard Le Gallienne*. Charleston, South Carolina: BiblioBazaar, BiblioLife, 2007.

Masters, Edgar Lee. *Spoon River Anthology.* New York City, New York: Macmillan, 1966.

McConnell, Addison Mitchell. "Nevertheless, she persisted." Rebuke of Senator Elizabeth Warren, US Senate Debate for Confirmation of Senator Jeff Sessions. Washington, DC: February 7, 2017.

Murphy, Joseph. *The Power of Your Subconscious Mind.* Radford, Virginia: Wilder Publications, 2007.

Oliver, Mary. "The Journey." In *Dream Work.* Boston, Massachusetts: Atlantic Monthly Press, 1986.

Oliver, Mary. "The Summer Day." In *New and Selected Poems.* Boston, Massachusetts: Beacon Press, 1992.

Ortiz, Ernesto. *The Akashic Records: Sacred Exploration of Your Soul's Journey Within the Wisdom of the Collective Consciousness.* Pompton Plains, New Jersey: New Page Books, The Career Press, Inc., 2015.

Ruiz, Don Miguel. *The Four Agreements.* San Rafael, California: Amber-Allen Publishing, Inc., 1997.

Twelve Steps and Twelve Traditions. New York City, New York: Alcoholics Anonymous World Services, Inc., 1976.

Wordsworth, William. "The World Is Too Much with Us." Poetry Foundation. Accessed March 31, 2020. https://www.poetryfoundation.org/poems/45564/the-world-is-too-much-with-us.

"You Can Get Anything You Want at Alice's Restaurant." *Off the Path from New York to Boston.* WSHU Public Radio, NPR News and Classical Music, November 22, 2019. https://www.wshu.org/post/you-can-get-anything-you-want-alices-restaurant#stream/0.